The
Battered Parent and
How Not to Be One

THE BATTERED PARENT AND HOW NOT TO BE ONE

James O. Palmer, Ph.D.

Prentice-Hall, Inc., Englewood Cliffs, New Jersey

Book designed by Joan Ann Jacobus
Art Director: Hal Siegel

The Battered Parent and How Not to Be One by James O. Palmer, Ph.D.
Copyright © 1980 by James O. Palmer, Ph.D.

Library of Congress Cataloging in Publication Data

Palmer, James O
    The battered parent and how not to be one.

    Includes index.
    1. Parenting. 2. Children—Management. I. Title.
HQ755.8.P34   649'.1   80-16432
ISBN 0-13-072371-1

This book is dedicated to the many troubled
parents who share their experiences with me.

Acknowledgments

I shall be ever grateful to Florence Franklin who initially and continuously encouraged me to write this book and who introduced me to that scholar and gentleman, Alex Jackinson, who saw that it got published.

Contents

The
Battered Parent and
How Not to Be One

1. BATTERED PARENTS AND HOW THEY GET THAT WAY

There are perhaps as many methods of rearing children as there are different societies and cultures. Traditionally, however, parents have been autocrats, demanding immediate and complete obedience from their children, with children having little or no say in family affairs. This traditional form of child care emphasizes *forms of discipline*: corporal punishment, guilt, shame, and the fear of God. Many American parents still practice the traditional autocratic approach to child rearing. The motto "Spare the rod and spoil the child" is still part of the Puritan heritage.

Not that children were never rebellious or willful prior to the twentieth century, but in very primitive societies, the child who dawdled on the jungle trail was in real danger of being lost or eaten by a wild beast. In the forest primeval, immediate obedience was a life-and-death necessity. Western children were warned of the horrors of disobedience through fairy tales such as that of Hansel and Gretel, in which self-indulgent children were in danger of being eaten by witches.

It is no accident of history that a more democratic approach to child rearing developed largely after the North American colonies rebelled against European tradition and later under the influence of the westward migration of the nineteenth century. As Margaret Mead has pointed out so well in *And Keep Your Powder Dry,* it has become the American tradition to break with tradition. Americans preach that every individual should choose his or her own vocation, own mate in marriage, and own politics. The Bill of Rights is given at least lip service by the people and the courts. As each young generation moved westward and formed new families of its own, it became a tradition to be independent, to develop a new trade from that of their fathers, new politics (such as the Republican Party), even new religions.

In the past three generations, particularly in the United States, there has developed what might be called a democratic approach to child rearing. Independence of mind is considered a value in democratic society, but a deviation in totalitarian cultures. Any all-powerful ruler wants obedient citizens; a democratic society requires citizens who think for themselves. To implement this ideal, American parents have gradually begun to permit their children to argue with them, to assert their own feelings and ideas, even to be a bit disobe-dient. Americans boast that their children have a will of their own. The ideal American child was never a Little Lord Fauntleroy, but a Tom Sawyer or a Penrod.

In modern-day America (and, in fact, the rest of the Western world), it is very difficult to utilize autocratic meth-ods or to expect a traditionalist child. Even if the child really does respond immediately, he gradually becomes more and more restless and rebellious. The fate of the traditionalist parent in our democratic society is often heartbreakingly severe. Whereas formerly children used to react to traditional parenting by having psychosomatic symptoms, by failure, or by showing other signs of passive resistance, now children openly revolt against traditionalist approaches in almost violent fashion. Especially after the youthful rebellion of the 1960s, there is little sanction left in American society for the traditionalist approach.

Children are now supposed to be disciplined by praise rather than punishment, and are encouraged to be independent and self-reliant. The democratic approach to child rearing emphasizes the *results* of discipline: feelings of self-worth, pride, self-confidence, achievement, and social respect.

But when one set of practices is disowned, the new approaches too often are not yet fully understood, leaving a limbo in which there are no commonly accepted rules. During a period of upheaval, practices may swing from one extreme to the next. Thus, the same community that sets up police protection for battered children may well vote—in democratic fashion—to allow teachers to spank their pupils. Even child psychiatrists—the shamans of child rearing—are terribly inconsistent; their speeches and books preach the importance of emotional supportiveness and reason, but in certain mental hospitals schizophrenic children have been disciplined with electric cattle prods. No wonder many American parents express feelings of doubt and confusion about child-rearing practices. Most have abandoned the traditional autocratic approach. They want to rear independent, creative children who will be free from guilt, shame, and fear. Yet they also want children to develop self-control, respect one another's rights, and be sensitive to other people's needs.

Although the current generation of parents is probably coming closer to achieving such goals than previous generations ever have, many parents still do not understand a democratic approach to child rearing or are unable to practice such an approach. This syndrome of what I call "the Battered Parent" (psychologically battered—not physically injured), is marked by at least four different signs or symptoms:

1. confusion as to who is in charge;
2. a generalized feeling of pain and depression on the part of the parent toward child rearing;
3. poor communication, typified by a great deal of screaming—or silence;
4. a seemingly perverse inability of both parents and children to recognize that anything is wrong in the family.

Battered Parents no longer attempt an autocratic rule over the child, but they have not as yet learned how to discipline, guide, and relate to children on any other basis. As will be seen much more clearly in later chapters, such parents misconceive the "democratic" approach as consisting largely of a passive indulgence of the child's desires. Since these parents confuse discipline with punishment, they misconceive democratic child rearing as lacking discipline. Battered Parents fear that instilling self-control would squelch their child's "ego," not understanding that children attain independence only gradually.

The Battered Parent in effect abandons the parental role out of despair and depression. As a result, a child who needs direction and guidance, who is relatively helpless and cannot take charge or be entirely independent, gives his parents a hard time, demanding that they take charge. As will be seen later, this "hard time" takes many forms, depending on the age of the child and the issue at hand.

The parents' battering is chiefly psychological, seldom physical. Only rarely do children physically attack parents or parents permit their children to physically abuse them. A child is far too dependent upon his parents to take the risk of harming them. Patricide is still much less common than infanticide—and when it occurs, is more often in retaliation against tyrannical, abusive parents.

All parents, even those whose child rearing is fairly democratic, are at times rejected or verbally attacked by their children. But the conflicts between Battered Parents and their children are more frequent and more extreme. Nearly all parents indulge a child's whims once in a while, even though they may know that this is not "the best thing" for the child. Similarly, many children talk back or at least manifest some kind of passive resistance to parental demands. However, in the battered-parent syndrome, these behaviors are commonplace.

"WHERE DID WE GO WRONG?"

Many psychologists, ministers, and educators insist that such parents are to blame, and many well-meaning and sincere parents do blame themselves when their children fail, get into trouble, or fall ill. Most parents feel that they share some responsibility for their child's development and reason that if things don't turn out well, it must be their fault. Certainly, parents do have a major responsibility, but the parent who bows his head in shame and confesses guilt often does no more to solve the problem than the parent who blames others.

Moreover, parental guilt often leads to depression and inaction: Self-blaming parents are likely to use their mistakes as a proof of inadequacy and an excuse to evade any further responsibility. The father who says, "I know I should have spent more time with my son" is likely to add, "but now it's too late, of course." The mother says, "Well, I guess I did spoil him a bit." Then she adds, "but I've never been a forceful person." Self-blaming is of no avail if it results in throwing up one's hands in helplessness.

Similarly, family counselors gain nothing by pointing an accusing finger at parents, who are then likely to become defensive and retreat. Novitiate or amateur counselors are likely to condemn the parent who won't "confess." Hearing confession is best left to the priests. Psychologists should stick to helping people think things through.

In particular, psychologists should help parents realize that accepting the responsibility for change is not necessarily the same thing as accepting blame. All of us, psychologists included, are far too much in the habit of searching out the *causes* of problems rather than their *solution.* Blame or guilt seldom motivate people to change a situation. They are primarily motivated when they hurt. Thus, parents in trouble need first to recognize that they are in psychological pain. Then, without blaming anybody, they need to be able to change as much as possible the child's behavior, their own behavior, and the situation and circumstances. The parent, along with the child, must accept responsibility for such change.

Notice that the child is included here too, since even small children have some responsibility for their own behavior. In fact, psychological growth consists largely in accepting increasing amounts of responsibility for oneself. Changing the situation requires a cooperative effort between child and parents. At times it may be necessary to exchange regrets and perhaps apologies, to acknowledge that errors were made. This recognizes that parents are human, parents make mistakes and have tempers; even that parents are selfish at times. *This* type of confession *will* help to clear the air, but does not divest anyone from the responsibility for change.

As Bruno Bettelheim has noted in his book *Love Is Not Enough,* parenting requires a continued alertness, an awareness of the child, an insight into what we are doing and into our own feelings. But once the regrets are exchanged, it is necessary to begin planning for the future. Perhaps a review of what has happened will help, so that the same mistakes will not be made again. Even more necessary, however, is to understand what needs to be done *positively.* With this increased awareness, a parent may anticipate problems and be there to head them off. Not that parents must be always anxious and protective, but they should be *prepared* with some moves, and plans and words of comfort or support.

Counseling usually consists of helping parents to become more aware of their child's needs and feelings. Most errors in child rearing are not sins of commission but of omission; usually parents find out what they should have done, might have said, might have understood.

Often parents' sleep is interrupted—if not by the child waking in the middle of the night, then by thoughts about how to solve certain problems.

All parents realize that parenting is hard work, with long hours, and that this is what gives them gray hairs and wears them down over the years. When you consider how much parents take, you may well ask why anyone bothers to have children at all. In the past, of course, many parents didn't really ask for children and had no way of planning what kinds of families they wanted. Many couples propagated without thought, or without realizing that it might be possible to avoid having children they did not want. But most people hope for children because being an effective and successful parent is a tremendous reward in itself. The hurts are balanced out by the affection parents receive from their children and the pride they have in them. Some hurts and disappointments of parenthood are so well-nigh inevitable, though, that you should really get ready to expect them.

I am inclined to believe that in child rearing there is always a certain touch of sadness, a touch of disappointment, the passing fear of being abandoned or unappreciated. The normal tragedies of life cannot be avoided altogether, and in this book I have tried to spell out which they are. Parents do *not* need to end up battered. Many other problems and traps are avoidable—or can at least be alleviated.

2. SOME BRUISES THAT PARENTS CAN EXPECT FROM BABIES

PREPARING FOR PARENTHOOD

Not all the bruises and batterings parents endure are unnatural. In fact, child rearing is often an arduous, wearing task that exhausts parental endurance and patience.

Marriage counselors and others constantly advise young couples to think carefully about whether they are ready to assume this demanding, long-range assignment before they start a family. Parenthood includes not only economics and physiology, but also a heavy and continuous responsibility for someone else's life. Moreover, the young couple hoping to have children must also consider that this arduous responsibility will restrict their lives and limit their activities.

At one time, children that parents really did not want or were not really able to care for properly were an almost unavoidable hazard of marriage. However, as various contraceptives have become more acceptable, the possibility of planned parenthood does approach reality. Unfortunately, births in most families still occur in haphazard and unplanned fashion. Yet even in the United States, there is enormous resistance to teaching planned parenthood in the public schools—or in any other approved institution. The press treats planned parenthood as a debatable controversy, suggesting implicitly that there is something sacred about unplanned conceptions. In fact, the unmarried teenager who becomes pregnant out of wedlock probably gets more advice and counseling about having a child (and *not* having a child) than does the average married woman.

Classes on planned parenting certainly should include some discussion of how mature persons should feel before they attempt to have children. If young people realize that they still want to do some growing, they might wish to delay having children for that reason alone. A lack of self-assurance or self-confidence should be a warning signal that entering parenthood might be quite hazardous. Admittedly, being a parent does force a young person to grow emotionally, but the shift from adolescence to young adulthood has to be accomplished before parenthood.

It is possible that a person can open up and become more affectionate once he or she enters into marriage and becomes a parent. On the other hand, the individual who tries to utilize marriage and parenthood to resolve interpersonal conflicts may find both the marital and parental relationship unstable. A marital partner might understand the anxiety that any exchange of affection can cause, but an infant senses only the anxiety. Premature parenthood can actually *delay* a young adult's maturation. Similarly, any hang-ups about cleanliness should be resolved before one starts off on the career of parenthood. As recently as the turn of the century, older children in a family participated a great deal more in the care of infants than they do today. Thus, many young women and even boys knew how to change a diaper or fix a bottle for their younger brothers and sisters. Unfortunately, such home training in infant care is now rather rare, though some public schools have held experimental classes in which teenagers of both sexes practice caring of infants and thus overcome any squeamishness they might have.

Even before a child is born, the growing fetus's very existence in the womb is a physical burden on the mother. Quite apart from the medical costs and other economic burdens that accompany the birth of a child, the very delivery itself is a painful as well as joyous event. Thereafter, the newborn makes a twenty-four-hour demand on his parents (which it is to be hoped both partners share). All the child's life functions—eating, disposal of wastes, and satisfaction of all creature-comforts—must be borne by the parents.

In most instances, the pride of creation and the joy of a new life outweighs these very natural burdens. Although some argue whether mothering is a natural instinct, at least most cultures teach women to believe that bearing and caring for a newborn is to be a joy. Any feelings of rejection or even of mild displeasure toward a newborn child are taboo. Yet there is considerable research evidence that most mothers probably harbor some negative feelings. Moreover, a fair-sized minority of mothers may not be completely delighted over the birth of a child and none too secretly regard it as an additional burden.

For example, a young woman who married while still in her teens and has a child soon after (especially one who married because she was pregnant) may be very poorly prepared to endure the tribulations of everyday child care. Young mothers may have very natural "nesting" instincts, but often they do not distinguish the live baby from the dolls they played with only a few years before. Not only do the diapers pile up, but the child's very existence becomes a severe restriction of its mother's freedom. There is less and less time for the teenage mother to be as carefree and footloose as she might like. Although she may comply with society's demands that she work hard at meeting the baby's needs, it is often very difficult for her to bury her resentment entirely. If she has another child and a third in rapid succession before she is twenty-five, she may become quite openly depressed. (What is even more tragic is that such haggard and depressed women are far more apt to be deserted by their husbands.)

Nor are older mothers immune to such natural bruises. The first child may be quite welcome, but the mother may hold a secret grudge against a second unplanned child that comes too rapidly thereafter. Two sets of diapers at once may overload not only the washing machine, but the mother's endurance as well. Sometimes the last child in a large family breaks the camel's back, but it is not unusual, on the other hand, for a woman to want a final child after she seems to have borne several more than her share. The child who arrives in the middle of the mother's childbearing years or is perhaps next to the last may seem to be the extra burden. Many mothers seem to pick out a child who represents to them the difficulties of child rearing, and for reasons of their own, project onto that particular child all of child-rearing's negative aspects.

I have emphasized maternal attitudes so far, largely because the bulk of child rearing traditionally falls on the mother's shoulders. However, it is equally common for a father to pick out a child whom he sees as representing an extra burden. It may be the same child the mother has focused on, particularly if he sees the child as a disturbance to the mother. In many families where there are a number of children, however, each parent may have his or her own black sheep.

In the traditional authoritarian family, such children often receive the majority of the punishment and blame. Naturally, the black sheep develop some kind of defense system with which to fight back. If they live to adolescence, they are likely to run away or be expelled from the family. But in the democratic family, negative feelings toward children are disallowed, creating guilt in the parents. The black-sheep child is never openly recognized as such, but rather becomes an uncontrolled offspring who batters his parents.

SOME BRUISES PARENTS ASK FOR, AND COULD AVOID

No doubt all parents have their lazy or careless moments. Some habitually negligent parents give their infant only the barest, sometimes insufficient, attention. Far more common is the parent who becomes overanxious about caring for the baby. Insofar as parents accept parenthood at all, they are generally eager to do a good job of it—often so eager that most parental errors arise from their very natural anxieties.

Consider, first, the baby whom both parents have been anxiously expecting. The couple may have been hoping desperately for a child, so much so—especially if the parents are thirty years of age or older—that it becomes the very center of their lives. They devote all resources, time, and energy to this only child, and their anxiety is heightened since they see it as an extension of themselves. Such parents try their best to change everything to suit the child's development. Where they live, how they live, even their jobs becomes dependent on what they believe the child's needs to be. Sooner or later they find that—as is usual in the battered-parent syndrome—the child is in charge.

Young parents, not quite sure of themselves, worry if they are going to do the right, "adult" thing. Again, there is the guilt that stems from the recognition that no baby is completely welcome, and many parents fuss unduly over their children in order to make up for their own guilty feelings about not wanting the child wholeheartedly. Parents may also have rigid feelings about cleanliness, only to find that babies present them with an unending parade of soiled diapers. Last but not least, parents may be overly eager to give all the love and affection which they themselves never got—or think they didn't.

Of course many anxieties seem unavoidable. There are disturbing events in everyone's lives; no one can avoid all the tragedies. Quite often mothers and fathers run up against the death of their own parents. Family finances rise and fall, marriages can get rocky at times, but since such hazards and misfortunes cannot entirely be avoided, it is essential that parents achieve a level of maturity that lets them handle these anxieties with sufficient calm and not disturb their children unduly.

Long before there was a science of psychology, it was recognized that infants sense and respond to anxiety. But many parents—and psychologists—continue to forget this basic fact of parent-infant relationships. As the parent tenses with anxiety, the child responds in kind. When parents are relaxed and at ease, usually the child is too. In fact, most of the behavioral problems of infancy are thus associated with parental anxiety. If a baby is not eating correctly, parents should first look to see what they are uptight about. The whimpering, upset, poorly functioning, "colicky" baby is—in adult terms—having an anxiety attack. Depressed mothers often find their babies either sluggish (from depression) or whimpering and sleepless. Even some of the illnesses from which infants suffer seem to occur when their parents are upset about outside pressures.

Establishing a reasonable schedule for both parent and child is one of the best ways to handle parental anxiety. Only a few years ago psychologists were advocating the "demand schedule" as the only way of avoiding frustration on the child's part. Parents were supposed to satisfy the infant at the moment, without any regard to their own needs. Such demand scheduling was a reaction to the previous style of child rearing, which had advocated a tight and regulated schedule with no regard to the particular child's needs. The child-rearing books of the 1920s and 30s outlined a precise timetable for training that was almost impossible to achieve. However, the "on demand" schedule of the 1940s and 50s was really no schedule at all.

Fortunately, there is a natural biological rhythm for feeding, sleep, and defecation that can quite easily become fairly regular schedule. In the first few months of life, schedule runs rather rapidly: The child's schedule of sle feeding has to be repeated several times over a twenty-four hour period—in contrast to the adult, who sleeps six to eight hours, eats meals quite a few hours apart, and can go a full six to eight hours without defecation. Initially, then, the parent must adapt to the child's more rapid schedule, but this *is* to be seen as a schedule. Thus, the parents can regulate the rhythm of the child's life even in the first few weeks, as most parents know, but not beyond the child's physiological possibilities. It is necessary to schedule a number of feedings, allow for numerous naps, and take care of the child's frequent bowel movements. But most parents find that they can very naturally and easily make these events conform to a rhythm, so that within the first month or so, child care forms an almost natural schedule.

Gradually, the 2 A.M. feeding and the 5 A.M. feeding coalesce. The baby awakens at certain times. The regulation of defecation does not seem to occur quite as rapidly, but parents soon know when to expect that the diapers will need changing. By only slight maneuvers on the parents' part, the newborn will adapt rather quickly to their needs and schedules. With only a slight delay or slight advance each day, the baby will soon adapt to the mother's rhythm.

A little natural hypnosis is often helpful, as has long been known to every parent who rocks the child. Rocking and cooing, talking and singing, lifting and setting down of the child in a rhythmic fashion is practiced by parents all around the world. Long before there were transistor radios, mothers sang and other members of the family added rhythm with musical instruments while the baby was being cared for. The very breathing of the mother helps establish a rhythm for

and natural scheduling of the infant's essary basic factor in child train-ablishes from the beginning that er than a one-way street. Such a itarian conditioning, à la Pavlov or

Watson, or a passive yielding to the child's demands. From such a rhythmic scheduling, a child learns that it will be supported, fed, and cuddled regularly and without fail. This instills the basic feeling of trust that Erik Erikson has demonstrated to be so essential to all future life relationships.

Scheduling infant care cannot be done in a rigid and impersonal manner. Sufficient food, warmth, and bowel and bladder care are vital necessities to the newborn, but as Harlow has shown with his motherless infant monkeys, cuddling and tactile contact—personal affection and "tender loving care"—are equally essential for infant development. When children's psychological needs for affection are seriously neglected, the detriment to their future development is often greater than if their physical needs were not fully met. A great deal of evidence shows that even those children who are frequently hungry, cold, or unprotected from the elements seem quite happy as long as they feel loved. Children starved to the point of malnutrition may actually become depressed, of course, but children who are fed and cared for adequately but perfunctorily and without any show of affection become severely depressed and may even die.

By establishing such an interchange of schedules in infancy, a host of problems may be at least ameliorated in later life, if not avoided altogether. One example occurs in toilet training. An infant *can* be conditioned to withhold feces and deposit them in the potty at an extremely early age. When infant conditioning was in fashion, parents used to boast of achieving this even before ten or twelve months. However, it is very difficult for a child to have effective bowel control before learning to sit up, and it is much easier when the child can walk to the potty. Some speech is often helpful ("Mama wants baby to go potty"). It is when the mother is in a great hurry, or feels that she cannot make any demand on the child whatever, that trouble begins. Once Baby finds that Mother can be disturbed by irregularities in the schedule, even the youngest infant may begin to take advantage of such control over the adults. Instead of defecating in the potty, babies may soil in the diapers with an almost vicious smile on their face. It takes considerable amount of parental persistence to keep at the task of training and scheduling. In too many instances a struggle develops between child and parent over bowel control; the parent is determined to show the child who's in control, and the child is equally determined to resist. However, if a parent does not enter into a battle for control, there is little problem.

Effective control of the bowels is much easier when the child is prepared in other ways: The basis for toilet training occurs in the first year of life, when parents schedule events to the rhythm of the body. Long before formal toilet training begins, the child will usually defecate at certain times of the day. The initial toilet training usually consists of putting the baby on the potty in time. If a parent observes these very natural body rhythms and takes advantage of them, formal toilet training becomes quite easy. Toilet training at somewhere between eighteen and twenty-four months is much more convenient for both parent and child—and, in fact, if not terribly inconvenient to the parent, could be delayed even further. At the same time, such parent-child interchange forms the basis of all future parental guidance and discipline. It takes into account the child's needs and abilities so that the child feels little or no strain but senses an order in the world; a regulation and a rhythm. At the same time, the parent—in control of the situation—can be relaxed and at ease with the child, who feels supported by this timed control. *The needs of the parent and child are both considered.*

Rearing an infant occupies a considerable amount of time and energy, and the initial months can be very draining physically and psychologically, especially if the task falls almost entirely on the mother—as it has traditionally. If the mother must neglect the child to wait on the father and satisfy his needs when he comes home, this intolerable form of neglect often leads to a parent being battered. If the father is an old-fashioned "macho" authoritarian who expects his wife to be his servant and give his needs the highest priority, then rivalry will quickly develop between him and the child.

Although fathers are often stronger and can bellow more loudly, most children know how to make such a father equally miserable. The child who is *truly* neglected may retreat initially, but will eventually find ways of retribution. Such a child often develops somatic complaints that give the mother an excuse to give them some priorities. Or if the pressure is greatest on the mother, *she* may develop the somatic illnesses. When father and child battle for care and attention, the child may become naughty or destructive, causing the father to demand that the mother take care of "her" child. This way, the child will have some attention—which is what she or he was aiming at in the first place.

Fortunately there is a growing trend for fathers to take up a considerable amount of the slack. For the male parent to share in the care of the newborn is good practice and also psychologically sound. From the very beginning he thus establishes himself as an equal parent, a partner with his wife in the job of child rearing. He is able to relieve his wife somewhat so that she can regain her physiological and psychological strength. When parents share in infant care from the very beginning, there is much less chance that they will end up battered. They will be united in their responsibilities toward their child and be able to work out any differences that may exist between them. Moreover, the woman's acceptance of the child is likely to be much greater if she sees her husband sharing in its care.

Furthermore, in today's world many women are establishing lives for themselves beyond the role of wife and mother. Child-care sharing strengthens the marriage and adds to a woman's feeling of worth and importance. Since in over 50 percent of families the wife has to work whenever possible, the father's participation will help the mother regain her strength and return to a paying job much more quickly. When she returns to work, moreover, she will continue to have her husband's support in the care of the child.

If the father is the main breadwinner, however, working outside the home for many hours of the day, he usually cannot manage to take equal care of the child; the greater part of the burden will continue to fall on the mother. As society progresses, it may be possible for fathers to have paternity leave, but a mother can have a daily "time out" if the father pitches in for at least a share of child care during the hours that he's at home.

Merely sharing anxieties often helps alleviate them. When we know that other people understand and are willing to lend a hand, the task provokes less anxiety. Suppose, for example, that a young mother would like to breast-feed her first child. Anxiety can often shut off the flow of lactation; the milk does not flow easily when the mother is tense. But the mother who knows that she will be aided in other ways may be able to relax and feed her baby much more easily. Her husband's devotion at this time may be of double importance. The fact that he shares in her anxiety even indirectly may be all that is necessary.

Even if misfortune and loss do befall parents, the resulting effect on an infant need not be disastrous. It is usually very helpful for people to have someone who can give some emotional support when they are experiencing a tragedy. In case of death, many people turn to their religious leader, to best friends, and to other members of one's family. Other people or agencies can help those in financial distress. It is a good idea to get some help in infant care when laid low by some misfortune.

If a parent is under stress, it is also wise to delay any changes in the child's habits or the start of any kind of training. For example, it would not hurt to delay the weaning of a child from the bottle when a mother does not feel up to this task. Toilet training in particular should not be attempted when parents are depressed or distressed. Scheduled events can be delayed or accelerated depending upon the parents' own needs—always, of course, keeping in mind the limits of the child's ability.

Very often when the child resists parental demands, he or she learns another fact of social life—namely, that parents get angry. Some parents become very guilty about being angry at their disobedient children; they would rather play little games and get the child to defecate at the proper moment, at the proper spot. But when the child continues to resist toilet training, it may be equally effective for a mother to display some degree of anger, just as she should show pleasure and praise the child for success in such an act. It does a child no harm to learn that parents can be displeased when she or he doesn't comply with their wishes.

Such expression of parental displeasure and anger should, of course, be in proportion to the act—and restricted to it alone. Parents can easily (and naturally) convey to their child that they are sick and tired of diapers. They should be careful that they don't add in other angers in their displeasure with the child. For example, if a woman is equally sick and tired of her husband arriving home late from work, it is not appropriate to add that anger into whatever displeasure she feels about her child's toilet habits.

THE RIGHT WAY TO NEGLECT A CHILD

One essential ingredient in the battered-parent syndrome is the attempt to provide complete, continuous, "wall to wall" love. Since a newborn must be waited on hand and foot (or rather mouth and anus) for many months, parents get into the habit of anticipating their child's needs almost before he or she asks. But when children's needs are met immediately and they encounter little or no frustration, they will grow to demand constant attention and affection. Thus, if for no other reason than to help children learn to begin to wait for satisfaction, a parent *must* begin to neglect them now and then. In fact there are many unavoidable situations in which a parent *must* make a child wait for satisfactions—or be at least mildly frustrated.

A child's needs cannot always be met immediately. When parents have other things to do for the moment, the child may have to wait briefly to be fed or diapered. Usually, some adult is readily available to pick up the child and cuddle him, but even in the early years of life, the child may have to spend a few moments alone with no one there to pick him up or give him a hug right away. Although a baby may come first in parents' attention and affection during waking hours, they have other obligations and pleasures. Gradually, they should expect the child to answer a few of its own needs.

Such neglect may take the form of passive actions—letting the child wait to be fed, or waiting a few moments to have his or her diapers changed. Gradually, however, a more positive form of neglect develops, such as toilet training or teaching children to feed themselves. Most of children's resistance to self-reliance comes from their almost instinctive fear that if they do take care of their own needs, they'll miss out on parental attention. Toilet training means that children have to do something for themselves *without* parental attention. Feeding themselves means they don't have a parent right there and then. Dressing themselves means that they can be without a parent for a while. However, the wise mother makes all this very palatable by constantly praising and encouraging self-help. When children see how proud a parent is when they put on their own shirt, then the underlying neglect will not seem as great.

Nevertheless, children usually have a residual yearning for those days when mother put their pajamas on, when she washed their faces for them, and they didn't have to do anything for themselves. Every once in a while, the normal preschool child will become ever so slightly helpless in the hope that mother will return to complete care. If mother *does* relent, of course, the feigned helplessness increases, and she can be battered into submission.

This does not mean that parents should refuse to give children a hand with the buttons that little fingers are not yet well coordinated enough to handle, or tie the laces they have not yet learned to tie. When a child is ill, a return to complete care may be warranted—temporarily. But frequent illnesses (such as alleged allergies, etc.) often become a form of assault. Every parent who has had an "asthmatic" child knows what it is to be forced to give in. Much asthma has been alleviated by a parent who says, in effect, "Yes, I'm sorry you're sick, but you still have to put on your own pajamas." Parents *do* have to kiss bruises to make them better, and put medicine and Band-Aids on cuts. Yet they also have to teach children how to be more careful to avoid such injuries, and how to take care of them independently when they do occur.

Such parental neglect may take the form of little "vacations" between mother and child. Once in a while, mothers need weekends off and time with their husbands away from the children. Unfortunately, reliable and willing caretakers are difficult to find, for the live-in grandmother or single auntie is now uncommon. Perhaps the formal profession of child-care assistance is needed, either in the form of nursery homes or people on call who are reliable and well trained. But in the meantime, the best a parent can do is to trade off so that mother gets an occasional holiday. Working mothers do get away and must find other agents to care for their children while they work. What needs emphasis here is that none of these forms of "neglect" really harm the child at all—unless, of course, the infant's needs (particularly for affection) are not met when the mother *is* present. This all presumes that children's needs are met regularly and fully, and that they have to wait only brief periods at times before they're satisfied.

3. SEPARATION ANXIETY AND THE RIGHT WAY TO GET ANGRY

Most children develop what Erik Erikson calls the "basic trust"—the sense that eventually there will be someone there to help them out and take care of their needs. As long as children possess that basic trust, they can separate from their parents for longer and longer periods of time. A child can spend an hour in the playroom or an hour outdoors knowing that mother is available in the house. Thus a child comes to feel that should there be any problem, she or he will never be completely neglected.

Yet it is undeniable that the slight, gradual, *normal* neglect that takes place in any child's early life usually causes a mild but pervasive anxiety, even when counteracted by encouragement and support.

No one enjoys feeling lonely, and everyone fears having no one that he or she could really depend upon. This underlying anxiety—that satisfactions may not be present when needed—makes every child turn every once in a while to double-check that someone is really there. Children will run back in the house for a moment, peek in to see mother or father and return outdoors. After going to bed, a child will get up to get a glass of water—not because of thirst, but to make sure that parents do not disappear once the light is out. When a child leaves the home for nursery school, this trust becomes even more essential. Ever in the back of the child's mind is the question: Will mother really return? This is why many cooperative nursery schools ask mothers to take turns being present in the classroom for the 3- or 4-year-olds. When it is necessary for mother to leave home to go to work, such separation anxiety becomes more intense.

Perhaps children were more emotionally secure when they were reared by mothers who did not have to earn a living. Fifty to 100 years ago, people lived in small groups. When mothers first participated in working, it was usually nearby—on the farm, in the family store, or in some form of "cottage industry." Up until about 30 or 40 years ago, the mother who worked outside the home was still a rarity, and in such instances, a father also was present many more hours of the day. The basic trust among people, so characteristic of life in American small towns at the turn of the century, does seem to be diminishing now in our society; and unfortunately, as some sociologists have pointed out, it is quite probable that enforced separation from the family in early childhood leads toward greater emotional isolation and alienation among adults.

However, if in previous times children gained the security of mother being constantly in the home, they also remained much more under their parents' authority for many more years than they do today. Nowadays, if children learn to be separated from their parents quite early in life, it prepares them for an increasing amount of separation later. Perhaps new values will take the place of personalized, intimate trusting. On the other hand, the current generation of young adults recognizes a need for greater intimacy, and it is to be hoped that these aspects of human relations will not be lost, even if parents are forced to make their children independent earlier in life. Separation anxiety seldom interferes with a child's development; rather, it forms one element in the social bond that keeps the human family and the human race together.

As children mature and are able to care for themselves in many different ways, they actually experience a conflict: The more they do for themselves, the more they gradually lose their parents' doting care. This is the constant danger in growing up and becoming independent. A girl may be thrilled at riding the bicycle without a guiding hand, but she feels a quickening anxiety lest the parent *really* let go. If a boy learns to read, will the parent continue to read to him. If they can get a drink of water, will mother continue to rise and fetch things for them?

When psychologists first tried to specify what is meant by anxiety, they conceived of it as the fears of an *individual*. According to this definition, anxiety consists of fears of the unknown, which each individual develops from personal experience. In the last several decades, however, psychologists have become increasingly aware that the experiences that create anxiety are, for the most part, *interpersonal* relationships.

One does not experience anxiety in a social vacuum. People are anxious because of the way other people treat them—or at least the way they fear they may be treated. And most personal anxieties are experienced mutually with at least one other person. If one individual in a social interaction is calm and secure, it is unlikely that the other will experience much anxiety. As a matter of fact, if a person enters a situation feeling anxious and finds that everyone else is secure and calm, he or she is much more likely to recover from the initial jitters. Whether or not anyone is jarred by another person's fears (imaginary or real), of course, depends upon one's own mood at the moment and one's basic feelings of security and insecurity.

When the social interaction occurs between a child and an adult—especially a parent—the child will most likely reflect the adult's mood and general feelings of security. When an unsure child meets a confident and emotionally supportive parent, the child's anxieties can most often be quickly assuaged. On the other hand, when normally secure and confident children find a parent upset and anxious, they are likely to be at least temporarily shaken by the parental distress. Just as children learn everything else at the parent's knee, they learn of anxiety: the ways of coping with it or hiding it, and how to deal with anxiety in others.

But if most anxiety is learned in parent and child interactions, is separation anxiety *merely* something within the child? Will the child become anxious about being independent if you are not anxious about his independence?

SEPARATION ANXIETY—IN PARENTS

Of course, any layman can observe that when a parent is overly anxious about a child's abilities at self-care, the child is also more anxious and becomes helpless. The effects of over-anxious and overprotective parental care have been noted throughout history, but have been given special focus in the last thirty years in the United States. Mothers now lean over backwards not to be "overprotective."

Nevertheless, any parent usually feels some degree of separation anxiety, however mild, during the children's first several years. It may begin when children take their first steps, when they can go to the potty independently, when they mount the tricycle and ride around the yard separate from parental arms, and especially when they leave the parent's immediate care to enter nursery school or kindergarten. Why is such separation anxiety so common, even among the best of the most well-meaning parents? What is it that parents are anxious about?

As children become more physically and socially independent, a parent may fear (1) that the children will be hurt or neglected, (2) that they will be socially and emotionally out of control, and (3) that they will no longer need, or return, parental love and affection.

A parent's *primary* fear is that a child may be hurt in some way. If a parent lets go and lets the children walk, they may fall and skin their knees. If mother does not get up to give them a drink of water, children may fall, get hurt, and spill water all over the floor. Perhaps more bumps on the knee *will* occur if the parent does not hold on to the tricycle. However, most parents realize that bumped knees really cannot be avoided. (I remember having scarred knees off and on from age 3 to at least age 13.) A second major anxiety is the parents' feeling that as children become more independent physically and more self-confident socially and emotionally, they can now escape adult control. Certainly, there is no little truth behind this fear. If a mother busy with a new baby tries to tell her three-year-old what to do, the three-year-old can just run off.

Often when the parent is over-anxious, a contest develops between parent and child over who is in control. Four- and five-year-olds can learn to defy their parents by not crying when spanked. The more parents try to put their foot down and insist that the child be obedient, the more defiant the child becomes.

Separation anxiety is most prominent when children actually leave the home physically, as when they go to school. This separation anxiety is also heightened as children become adolescents, and again when they finally leave home to become young adults. Thus, separation anxiety usually reaches an initial peak when a child is somewhere between ages four and six. Parents who are anxious because their child is no longer a dependent infant will have increasing difficulty in teaching that child obedience. If parents recognize and are able to deal with a child's gradual increasing independence, then they will be firm and help the child develop self-control, modeled on what you request.

In other instances, worries that the child may not behave away from home are particularly characteristic of a parent who has anxieties about social conformity. The adult who depends on social approval, who fears nonconformity, may become particularly anxious as a child goes out in public. Somehow parents do not always trust the training they have given their children—but the child who is not trusted is the most likely to misbehave! The parent who says, in effect, "You're too little to understand, so you must do what I say," is very likely to meet with increased resistance. When children sense that anxiety lies behind a parent's demands, they will soon take advantage of the parental anxiety; and the parent who is anxious about the loss of control is most vulnerable of all.

On the other hand, the parent who says in effect, "I think you're old enough to behave in a socially approved way, and I expect you to control yourself," is less likely to meet with defiance and more likely to find the child trying to cooperate. Sometimes this approach takes the form of, "How come you're acting like a baby?" However, this kind of admonition does not quite support a child's efforts to be independent and yet still conform socially.

To gain a child's cooperation in social behavior, *praise* is the strongest form of discipline available. Thus, if a parent says, "I'm *very* proud of you for acting like a big boy (or big girl)," the child is most definitely likely to repeat the behavior of which the parent approves. Such praise must be appropriate and genuine, of course, but should be applied at every opportunity, no matter how slight the sign of desired behavior. Praise demonstrates that the parent feels confident that the child will still continue to grow and be even more socially effective. Parents who encourage children to be independent and tell them how proud they are of their abilities to care for themselves and control themselves emotionally and socially, will in turn be rewarded by independent, voluntary, and spontaneous expressions of affection.

When a child becomes more independent, the most basic parental fear that arises is of a possible loss of love. This fear is actually the core of the parent's unspoken anxiety that the child will not really need the parent anymore. A great deal of children's affection for their mothers and fathers derives from the fact that they need their care, physically and emotionally. The need for care is not the only basis for the affection between parent and child, of course. Usually this kind of bond is greatly strengthened and enhanced by the physical affection parents lavish on children even when they are not answering any other particular need. Thus, parents coo over a child and rock a baby in their arms even after it is satiated with food. Parents pet and tickle children after they've been bathed and diapered afresh. Parents tuck children into bed, and rock and sing to them even after they're physically warm and comfortable. A child may be engaged in some play activity, but parents are there, attentive and chatting; parents offer kisses and hugs even when the child is not hurt and is feeling quite happy.

Most children respond readily to all this: The parents get kisses and hugs back; the child shares with them his feelings and activities. But as the child moves on, riding the tricycle a little farther down the block, spending more time with another child in a nursery school or talking to a stranger, the parents get less and less of their child's attention and affection.

Usually this kind of separation happens very gradually. Parents may not even notice it at first. Perhaps they are preoccupied with a younger child who comes along just as the older one enters nursery school or kindergarten. Yet every mother (and perhaps many fathers too) has had a moment when she looks up and suddenly sees how much her child has grown, notices that she or he shakes hands instead of kissing goodnight. At that moment there is a quickening of the heart and a slight inner panic, a feeling of loss.

This kind of normal anxiety is so commonplace that few parents think anything about it. Yet there are also moments when children rush over and say voluntarily, "But Mother, I really do love you!" as if they realized at that moment that she needed some reassurance. Such parental anxiety becomes more of a factor when either parent is depending on the child for feelings of being needed and as a source of affection.

All parents can think of times when they actually turned to their children for emotional support. Such separation anxiety increases if parents are anxious about other things, or suffering other losses such as the death of a parent or marital dissent. Take, for example, an adult who has lost one of his or her own parents. The death of a grandparent usually upsets even a young child because the child realizes that mother or father is suffering the loss of a source of affection. In families where a grandparent has died, one often finds a short period of anxious interaction between parents and children. The parent may quite unconsciously be more demanding of the child who, sensing the parent's anxiety, may in turn feel insecure. Parents may wonder why the child seems to be misbehaving, right at the moment when they themselves are suffering. If parents can explain and share an open grief, however, their child will be much less disturbed.

Such insecurity is even more intense for the child when parents quarrel and separate, because the child fears a loss of the parent. Conversely, parents who have lost each other's love frequently make greater demands on the child and become anxious about the possibility of losing his affection. (This is the source of many custody battles.) Of course, marital dissension, separation, and divorce only increase normal separation anxiety.

Children reflect these anxieties and will do what the parents expect—for example, fail at school. Each parent can then blame the other because "your" child is failing; each points out that his or her ex-spouse is an inadequate parent who really cannot take care of the child. Each parent ignores the fact that the children could easily do the schoolwork and take care of themselves before the divorce occurred.

One of the far more common signs of separation anxiety occurs when either parent or child becomes overanxious about being angry at the other. Of course, many parents *are* afraid of being angry at their children—afraid that the child will in some way be hurt, at least psychologically. And they fear that the child will reject them—both their control and their love. But it is the parent who cannot permit the expression of anger who may most easily lose control of the child. Once, when I was discussing the problems of discipline in the classroom, one schoolteacher remarked, "Our principal says we should never hit a child in anger." Another, older teacher responded, "Are we supposed to hit them in cold blood?"

When a parent really wants children to do something and is upset and angry at their behavior but holds back the anger, children will nevertheless know that the anger is really there. Moreover, they may have serious doubts as to whether the parent really means what he or she says. If a mother wants her child to come in the house and says, "Dear, please come in the house, won't you?" the child may dawdle. If she says, "Darling, please come in and don't make mommy angry," the child may continue to dawdle—because when a parent behaves in a perfectly calm fashion when it would be reasonable and natural to be angry, the child is usually aware that the parent is repressing anger. However, if she follows this up by saying, "I am going to count to five, and at this point, I will make you sorry you didn't come in the house," and says it in a loud, firm voice, most likely the child will pay immediate attention to the request.

On the other hand, the parent who fears the child's anger often becomes a victim of it: If a mother or father fears that children's anger indicates a loss of love, then the children can easily take advantage of the parent by snarling at every opportunity.

Recently, I watched a parent and child leaving kindergarten. The boy was shouting at his mother, "You're just plain mean—plain mean, that's all, plain mean." "I really don't care," said his mother, glaring down at him, "I shall be mean if I need to be." She walked to the driver's side of the station wagon. The child struggled for a moment, was able to open the large and heavy car door on his own, and climbed in. The mother sighed, leaned over, and slammed the door shut.

Although this wasn't a pleasant scene, it did seem to me that neither mother nor child had any great anxiety about being angry. They could be *safely* angry at each other without fearing any great loss. The boy could get angry at his mother and not be afraid that she would abandon him. He seemed to be confident that he *would* be cared for when he needed it (as illustrated by the fact that his mother did close the door when he couldn't). Similarly, she could be angry back at him without fearing of making him overanxious. She also realized that he would probably continue to be somewhat independent, and thus permitted the sturdy little fellow to struggle with the car door. Thus, neither mother nor son was overly anxious about any loss of care, control, or affection.

One of the most common questions parents ask child psychologists is, "How can I allow my child to be impudent, to defy me, and yet maintain any kind of control or guidance?" The basic difficulty here is that many parents *themselves* have never learned to discriminate between words and deeds. Many people don't realize that the angry person does not *necessarily* follow up the words with an act of violence; nor does one person's expression of anger have to arouse a defense in the other person. On many occasions, the response is in effect, "Oh, I'm sorry! I didn't know I hurt your feelings."

First, therefore, parents should accept for themselves that anger may be expressed *without* aggressive action. You have to learn to say to your child, "Yes, I understand you are angry. You have a right to be angry. But, no one's going to hurt you, and we're all taking notice of how badly you feel." At other times when the child is frustrated, a parent may have to tell children that, in the long run, they simply must accept their frustration.

This is especially true when children have to be denied something and feel potentially deprived. It often takes them some time to learn that they must await satisfaction. Most of all, a parent should learn to demonstrate to children in *actual behavior* that anger need not be met with anger. Say a child gets enraged at something a sibling did and comes stomping and screaming into the house. Once he or she discovers that parents don't necessarily respond with equal anger, but can remain calm, the child will calm down, and will begin to see that other people's behavior is not such a complete threat; that some satisfaction can be obtained, or compromises achieved. On the other hand, should a parent *fail* to get angry at an appropriate time, then the child may be very puzzled. The child who senses that parents cannot be angry will feel uneasy and often torment them all the more, hoping that they will express their feelings openly.

Expression of anger is a very important part of human interaction. Children have to learn that if they transgress other people's rights, they may very well meet with anger. Certainly they should learn that if an adult isn't obeyed, or is disregarded, then they will suffer a temporary loss of approval and affection. Thus, it is most important that learning about anger should begin in the parent-child relationship.

It *is* true that if parents scream frequently and loudly at their children, they will not obey any better than if spoken to too softly. This does not mean that an occasional scream cannot be quite effective, but then, screaming is not the only way to express anger. Quite similarly, a child should learn that his or her anger can be expressed and understood—and, to a certain extent, accepted. Parents should accept the fact that a child doesn't really want to obey them: the things they ask of a child may be interrupting, distasteful, or even threatening. Children may have other things they want to do rather than do the thing that a parent requires. All of this means that a child has a perfect right to be angry—but not the right to disobey. In fact, parents may well expect a child to be angry *and* obedient at the same time. When asked to come in the house, when they want to continue playing outdoors, they may well storm into the house momentarily quite angry. But children whose anger *is* accepted will get over it faster. A parent can expect them to cool down gradually, if not immediately.

4. UNDER- AND OVER- PROTECTION

Many child-guidance counselors use the term *overprotective* to indicate a parent worried excessively and unnecessarily about the child's welfare. The overprotective parent typically rushes in to make a decision, without consulting the child or taking his feelings into account. The overprotective parent sees danger in every move and is quick to push the panic button whenever the child's safety or health is threatened. The most common sign of overprotectiveness is constant worry that the child will fall sick.

In general, illnesses are the result of two conditions. The one that most people understand is when some germ, virus, or other toxic substance attacks the body. Anyone may yield if the invading substance is strong enough. Thus a massive invasion of a virus, germ, or poison, a crack on the skull or a bullet wound, may lay any one low. However, the degree of illness depends on the health of the body being invaded. A person whose resistance is low is more likely to catch poliomyelitis and find it much more difficult to recover from broken bones or wounds. *Emotional tension particularly lowers resistance.* This is most evident in the case of auto accidents, in which someone who is very tense is most likely to be injured. Emotional tension wastes precious energy and weakens the body, making it more susceptible.

A second main cause of illness—the least understood by both the public and the medical profession—results from misusing or overusing certain bodily functions. Among such ailments are stomach ulcers, hemorrhoids, and many types of skin disorders, commonly labeled "functional." If a person continually "swallows" anger, he is likely to end up with severe stomach problems as a form of emotional expression. Adolescents who become overheated by unexpressed sexual feelings are likely to have some skin problems. The person who chokes up with anger and disappointment often becomes asthmatic. No germ causes asthma, and it is very likely that most "allergies" are primarily of emotional origin. When allergens are present throughout the air, it is very difficult to explain otherwise why one person reacts and another does not.

THE REWARDS OF POOR HEALTH

In the so-called Puritan culture that has dominated American life for nearly three centuries, illness has long been the only acceptable excuse for not meeting one's responsibilities. Under the Puritan ethic, not to work is absolutely impermissible. It is equally impermissible to become angry. Children are expected to obey their parents unquestioningly. It is unacceptable to demand attention, unacceptable to be "emotional."

However, people can avoid work by the excuse of

illness. By being sick, they may legitimately demand service and attention from others. By being physically unable to leave the house, they can avoid unwanted social activities, and by being ill, avoid punishment for their sins. If God has punished someone by a handicap, that person may not need any other punishment.

The types of illnesses with which children victimize themselves and their parents are far more often of the functional type, but may well be "psychosomatic"—that is, illnesses caused by or expressive of emotional conflicts. Even though illness is often recognized as having an emotional component, *how* that component operates—especially between parent and child—is often not fully understood. Children and parents clearly attempt to relate in various ways and conditions through children's illnesses. Where emotional tensions are high in a family, a child may be susceptible to frequent infections. Often one child in the family will seem to catch everything and be dreadfully ill, *whereas* a brother or sister will be far more resistant—or, if he or she does succumb, the illness will be less severe. Should a child fall sick, the parent anxious over separation becomes even more uneasy. Often parents use a child's illness as an excuse for restricting the child's independence. And in this fashion, a child may learn that illness can be used to arouse parental fear and attention.

In a parent-child relationship, then, the chief reward for illness is the child's control of the parent. It is very difficult to deny anything to a sick child; in the past, the child who is always ill has been considered "frail." Thus, the child who has frequent colds, allergies, even repeated accidents, or has a prolonged illness that results in handicaps or limitations frequently can—and does—control his parents.

For example: Ricky was born on Ellen's 18th birthday, and it is likely that her pregnancy was the cause of the marriage: She and her husband David had been married only six months when Ricky was born. Ellen herself was ill during a great deal of her pregnancy, seemed quite depressed, and wept frequently, admitting to her mother that she wished she were not pregnant. However, Ricky's birth was quite normal and he seemed to be a healthy baby—at least initially. But it seemed to Ellen that her son Ricky had been asthmatic since birth, although his disorder was not labeled asthma until he was almost two. During the first two years of his life, he seemed to have a great deal of bodily discomfort. He slept fitfully, always seemed to have a stuffed-up nose, and found breathing difficult. He was a finicky eater and frequently vomited up what he ate. He cried at the least discomfort, and it was difficult to quiet him.

In the first two years of his life Ricky's illnesses occupied a great deal of Ellen's time and energy. Consequently, she had little time for her husband, who complained that often she was too tired for sexual relations. Besides, considering Ricky's condition, neither of them were eager to have another child right away. David was also a teenager and relatively unskilled. It was difficult for him to find or keep a job, and so the young family was frequently in dire economic straits. Ellen returned frequently to her mother for emotional comfort and to borrow money.

David began to spend less and less time at home and Ellen became aware that he was being unfaithful. When Ricky was about three, his father announced that he was leaving them. Ellen, quite depressed, returned to her mother, who lived on a small pension she had received after Ellen's father was killed in war. David supplied no child support and Ellen was forced to go to work.

It was at this time that Ricky's asthma became quite definite and severe. He was cared for by his grandmother, who delighted in cooking him special food, bringing him little presents, and reading to him by the hour. Occasionally David would visit them, but Ricky's asthma always grew worse after his father left. Ellen felt obligated to spend every spare minute with Ricky when she was not working. However, she was a pretty young girl who attracted men very easily, and men she met at work frequently invited her out on dates.

Every time she went out, Ricky would have a severe asthma attack.

His grandmother took him from doctor to doctor and he accumulated a large supply of different medicines. Because of his asthma he did not go to a nursery school, and his first attempt to attend kindergarten was followed by a night during which it seemed that he might die for lack of breath. By the time he was six, however, he had to begin to attend school—usually accompanied by his grandmother. Ricky did well in his lessons and thus was academically successful, for which his grandmother and mother gave him considerable praise. However, he remained somewhat isolated socially and never competed in any sports.

At this time his father was remarried to a woman with two boys, one a year younger and one a year older than Ricky, who was frequently invited to his father's home on weekends. The stepmother made fun of him, however, and it was obvious that his father enjoyed physical activities with his new sons in which Ricky could not participate. Gradually these visits with his father became less frequent and he was not pressed to return.

When Ricky was almost nine, his mother remarried. Ricky had met Floyd, his new stepfather, only once in his life, and it seemed to Ricky that no one had told him that his mother was going to marry him. Again Ricky's asthma became almost incapacitating. Floyd was a gentle man who appreciated that Ricky was chronically ill and did not pressure him in any way, but Ellen realized that Ricky's illness might well interfere with her adjustment with her new husband. Thus, she welcomed her mother's suggestion that Ricky continue to live with her while she and Floyd got started in a new home. Ricky visited his mother and Floyd almost every weekend, but it was on weekends that he had his most severe asthma attacks. His pediatrician thought that perhaps there was more pollen in the area where Ellen and Floyd lived than where his grandmother resided, and thus the visits became less frequent. Ellen was more likely to drop by occasionally to see her son and mother than to bring Ricky over to her new home.

Ricky's return to live with his mother was delayed again when Ellen became pregnant. A year after his half sister Dedee was born, Ricky was still living with his grandmother. Ellen felt very guilty at neglecting Ricky and having forced a special burden onto her mother. She realized that besides being asthmatic, Ricky was a petulant and demanding child who was thoroughly spoiled and had always had his own way. Thus, she was very unwilling to bring him into her new home, where she seemed to be finding happiness for herself for the first time in her adult life.

Ricky's grandmother became severely ill and died just before Ricky turned thirteen. For some time thereafter, he was quite ill himself. His asthma seemed so constant that he could not attend school and spent most of his time in bed. He spent a brief time at the hospital, where his entire health problem was reviewed. A counselor there advised Floyd and Ellen that a great deal of Ricky's asthma at the time represented his grief for his grandmother's death: He was, quite literally, "choked up." Ricky was a well-behaved boy who never gave anybody any trouble other than through his illness. He had soon found that if he threw a temper tantrum, his grandmother would reject him utterly. Whenever he felt angry thereafter, he had an asthma attack. The counselor advised the parents that they should let Ricky know that they recognized how very much his grandmother's death disturbed him and that Ellen might well share his grief.

This step did help Ricky enough that he could come home and return to school. The family continued to seek the aid of the counselor, who then advised that they discontinue the rewards that Ricky had derived from his asthma in the past. Of course the special care and attention he had received from his grandmother was no longer present in Ellen's home. When Ricky demanded special attention, he was kindly but firmly refused. On the other hand, when he engaged in healthy, normal, and outgoing activities, he was given praise and support. For example, he enjoyed going places with Floyd, who always invited him along whenever he had to run an errand. At times when Ricky was ill, Floyd would wave and say, "Well, tomorrow when you feel good, let's go again." Following the counselor's advice, Ellen left medicines that Ricky was free to utilize, but when he was ill, no one forced any medicine on him or gave him any special care.

Under this routine, Ricky's asthma cleared up fairly completely within a year. Only when he was tired or under special emotional pressure did Ricky have an asthmatic attack, and these were relatively light, for the most part, as compared with his severe attacks in early childhood.

Sometimes it is very difficult to recognize that an illness does spring out of the parent-child relationship. But once this is recognized, the possibility of dealing with the illness is much greater. Ricky's story illustrates how parents can avoid being victimized by illness. Children can use illness to control their parents in many ways, but if a parent refuses to be controlled, then this childhood tactic will not work any better than any other such attempts by children.

If the illness does not earn any reward for the child or any control over the parent, it is more likely that the child will begin to recover. Similarly, illness may be a way of expressing feelings, as when Ricky became so ill after his grandmother's death. Parents can also avoid being the victim of children's illnesses merely by recognizing the emotions that are being expressed through the illness. If parents can divine and accept the child's underlying feelings, then, again, it is likely that the illness will be ameliorated.

THE HANDICAPPED CHILD

If it is hard to recognize the role that parent-child relationships play in illness, it is usually even more inadmissible for parents to admit being burdened by a child who has a handicap. Certainly a child who is crippled, hard of hearing, blind, or retarded does need special care, which draws on parents' time, energy, and patience.

When it is discovered that a child is disabled, one of the first things a parent commonly asks is "Why did this happen to *me*?" This question occurs even to well-educated people who should be able to realize that tragedies happen quite often completely by chance. Yet the feelings of responsibility are often so strong that even when tragedies occur over which the parent could not possibly have any control, parents are likely to feel guilty: The child's least disability may seem like a curse. This attitude stems from the time when misfortune was considered punishment from God and people searched their souls to find what sin they had committed to deserve such chastisement. Thus, when a child has a disability, parents may begin to feel as if they had violated some commandment and the child might be a continued representation of their evil intents or deeds. Again, one would think that these attitudes had disappeared with the Age of Superstition, but psychologists report that such attitudes remain quite common even in modern society. Thus, the very existence of a handicap in a child may injure a parent because of the parent's own superstitions.

Actually what is being discussed here is a *disability*, and how much the disability will become a handicap, again, depends a great deal on how the child is treated. For example, there are children who are severely crippled, but who are not severely handicapped. They may get around much better and have fewer problems than other children whose physical limitations are actually much less. The degree of physical and social limitations imposed by the disability will depend upon what parents expect from the child and how much they allow the child to be a burden. At times, the amount of burden may depend upon the severity of the handicap. Yet how much of a burden a handicapped child may prove to be depends mostly upon the type of parent-child relationship established.

Even where little or no guilt is involved, a child's disability does cause parents extra grief and obligation. Any parent feels it necessary to try to do anything she or he can to make life easier for a disabled child. Such children can be spoiled, however, and made more helpless by the parent's very efforts. Such children, even more than physically normal ones, need continual encouragement to be independent and to utilize whatever abilities they may have. For example, a blind child—who must eventually find his way around the community as an adult—should be encouraged to find his way around the house, even at the risk of bumping into things. It may be necessary to keep everything in its place so that the blind child knows just where things are, and this will be a slight extra burden on the parent. With a blind child, it is also necessary to keep up a running conversation as to what is going on and where things are. Yet it is not necessary to do *everything* for the blind child, for this will actually make him more helpless in the long run. The special training outlined by the Association for the Junior Blind emphasizes the need for promoting independence in every way. Certainly the same is true of the child with any handicap: If at all possible, it must never be used as an excuse to get out of doing things that it might be possible to do with only a little effort.

Just as one need not be continually depressed over a handicap, but there is really no denying that it is equally unrealistic always to be cheerful. There will be times when it is impossible for the child to do something because of the handicap. Such moments may cause at least temporary sadness in both child and parent. Again, however, an open recognition of feelings by both parent and child will alleviate the situation. The limitation must be recognized *at the time*, with some sadness on both sides. Such occasional recognitions will actually limit the amount of grief in the long run. The wise parent will help the child compensate with other activities not restricted by the handicap, in which the child can find a greater success.

Parents who need to have a child succeed—and thus prove the parents themselves a success—may feel terribly victimized by a disabled child, especially if the child is intellec-

tually retarded. Mental retardation is perhaps the most difficult handicap to deal with, and the one that seems the greatest
tragedy in our society today. In the first place, it is difficult for
parents and children to admit that the handicap actually exists.
I have seen parents admit that they would much rather have a
child who is blind, deaf, or even psychotic than one handicapped by retardation. The professional people who deal with
retarded children seem to make up a new euphemism every
ten years or so. Some of the names once thought to be kindly
have now become perjoratives. For example, the label "fee-
bleminded" is never used anymore, even though objectively,
this term is no better or worse than any other. A far greater
misnomer is "the exceptional child," since many people unfa-
miliar with this term would take it to mean that the child was
very bright. This term masks the whole fact of retardation.
The current terminology of "developmentally disabled" or
"slow learner" does permit parents and children to accept the
handicaps without blame and to see them in terms of development and learning. Such terms help everyone avoid setting
achievement goals too high, while acknowledging the need
for special conditions to help the child learn and develop.

An example of how retardation need not be a severe
handicap is seen in the case of Billy. For four years his school
had put up with the fact that Billy was not completely toilet-
trained. At age ten, he was still wearing diapers and rubber
pants. His IQ, measured several times, had ranged from 65 to
75 depending upon the tests and the conditions of the examination. Thus, Billy was deemed "educable"; indeed, he
seemed quite normal when he spoke, and had a fair vocabulary, but was quite slow at learning the school tasks. He was a
pleasant, smiling, cheerful, socially outgoing child who was
quite acceptable to his peers except for the fact that he smelled
constantly of feces and urine. In fact, when the other children
called him "Stinky," Billy actually seemed unaffected and
smiled along with them.

At the end of the school year, the school authorities

informed Billy's mother that he wouldn't be readmitted in the fall unless he were toilet-trained. For counseling, they referred her to an agency that specialized in the care of the retarded. There it was discovered that Mrs. R. had always accepted Billy's lack of toilet-training as part of his disability and had made little or no effort to have him control his bowel and bladder. Mrs. R. had five other children, all older than Billy. When Billy came along "I thought I was through washing diapers, but I guess it's my fate in life," she laughed. During that summer, a special therapist worked with Billy and his mother just on his toilet-training problem. He was given special rewards when he used the toilet on his own and when he was dry during the night. On the other hand, when he soiled his clothes in the daytime, he had to wash them out and eat by himself. Within a few weeks he was almost completely toilet-trained.

Having established that he could control himself and do things on his own, his parents and siblings began to treat Billy as if he could be potentially normal. They no longer babied him but demanded he do his share of simple tasks around the house. He proved particularly adept in the garden, and for his activities there, his parents gave him praise as well as monetary allowance. At school, Billy learned to write his own name and recognize certain words in the book, but by the time he was twelve it was obvious that he was never going to be literate. He could count, but not make change. He could spell out words like "*stop*," "*go*," "*slow*," but he could not read a complete sentence.

At this time, the mother admitted to the agency therapist that her husband was also illiterate. This surprised the therapist, since the family lived in a nice home with a swimming pool, and Mr. R. obviously earned a good living. However, Mr. R. had never completed the fourth grade and had taken up plastering as a teenager. He had built a great deal of his own home, including the swimming pool, but Mrs. R. did all of his business accounts.

Shortly thereafter, with the therapist's encouragement, Mr. R. started taking Billy along with him on his work. By the time Billy was sixteen, he was a good plasterer and making a good living. (In fact, the therapist realized that Billy and his father together made more money than did she and her teacher husband!) Yet if it had not been for the intervention of the agency, Billy would likely have ended up a fairly handicapped adult who might have spent all his life in a state-supported institution.

It is perhaps difficult for most people to be proud of their retarded progeny, but parents of retarded children are gradually beginning to realize that it is a tremendous success if their child grows up able to utilize whatever abilities he may have and live as happy a life as possible. Rearing and educating a retarded child are very special tasks that demand a great deal from parents, and those who succeed in them may be justifiably proud.

With a focus on learning, parent and child can take the special steps that will give the retarded child the best possible training. As with any other disability, the parent must keep promoting as much independence as possible. Even the severely retarded can usually be toilet-trained and taught to dress and feed themselves, whether or not they develop any speech. Several decades ago, a national survey revealed that retarded children who were kept at home and given special care and guidance by their parents often were much less handicapped than those who were allowed to vegetate in hospitals.

Of course the mildly retarded child can often develop and be taught skills that may eventually allow him to be relatively independent and to earn a living. If parents can accept a retarded child with his limitations, if their expectations are appropriate to the child's ability, then it's entirely possible that the mildy retarded child can become a productive, relatively happy adult.

THE DEMOCRATIC PARENT

An overprotective parent protects children against their own impulses, rather than helping the child find socially approved ways to obtain satisfaction. But being an active, involved, and decisive parent does not at all mean being overprotective. On the contrary, the average child-guidance specialist would probably regard a Democratic Parent as almost *under*protective. Not that Democratic Parents aren't aware of all the exigencies bearing on a child, but such parents will allow a child to make independent decisions as often as possible, and are willing to take the chance that the child may make a mistake.

The Democratic Parent is not so much *permissive* as looking for situations where the child can try his wings. The Democratic Parent is cautious, thoughtful, and deliberate, but also encourages the child to practice being thoughtful and deliberate.

When something new comes up that the child has not done before on his own, the Democratic Parent is likely to say, "Let's look at all the facts first and then try it at least once." In all child development, there must be pilot attempts; moreover, parents must continually allow for at least minor goof-ups. Any child is likely to stumble as he learns to walk, fall off the tricycle or bicycle, or dent a fender in learning to drive. A child's initial speech is halting, she or he prints the first numbers backwards, the spelling is phonetic, the reading is imperfect. But all these risks have to be taken, if the child is to grow into an independent adult.

Usually the bumps aren't really as painful to the child as the bruise of having failed. Nor are they as damaging to the parent as the rise in blood pressure, the inherent panic suffered when a child takes such risks. Again, this is a normal, every-day worry that occurs continuously throughout parenthood. When children fail, it is, of course, necessary to comfort them and let them know that success is not expected immediately, or every time. If a child is trying something that might not be expected at that age, then say, as do the baseball fans, "Wait 'til next year." And when children succeed, they also need parental support, praise, compliments, and encouragement. Parents must let a child know every time that they are pleased, that they are happy for him or her, and enjoy the child's success—for success means nothing if there's no applause or smile of admiration. Even if no one else appreciates a child, the parents must.

MAKING THE BEST AND WORST OF THINGS

Despite anyone's best efforts to prevent them, accidents will occur without warning. Some tragedy is part of every life and to most of us it seems greatest when it affects our children.

At times unemployed or poverty-stricken parents are helpless to control their own finances, and are certainly not to blame altogether if they cannot supply the necessary essentials of life. If young parents make errors in judgment and their marriage turns out a failure almost from the start, this, too, is a tragedy for the child that maintaining such a marriage does not rectify.

Withal, there will also be real emergencies, times when parents must work swiftly and decisively, giving the child every support. These times allow little deliberation. If a child is in physical danger, parents do have to take immediate action. Other than physical danger, however, there are really very few true emergencies. Most social emergencies can and should wait.

Even in the physical emergencies, however, there need be no panic if parent and child together can think through the steps to be taken in advance. If, for example, a family lives in a part of the world where earthquakes or hurricanes can be expected, then they should plan what to do in case of such a natural disaster. Such training for emergencies was learned by people in Europe during World War II, and America had a taste of it when we first feared retaliation for the atomic bomb. In a calm moment, perhaps when the family have all heard of an accident and have it in mind, a parent needs to ask the child, "What should we do if you were injured in an automobile accident?" or "What might be done if I were injured?" Then discuss and outline the kinds of steps necessary to take, including keeping a cool head. Most children are fascinated by such discussions and feel much more assured to know that their parents *do* have emergency plans.

Perhaps the best you can do is to be aware of what kinds of tragedies can happen and do your best to prevent them. Here, again, the active, concerned, involved parent is usually the least likely to suffer. Such a parent can be there to haul children out of the street, take them to playgrounds where they are safer, to see that they have swimming lessons, to guide them on their bicycles, and even argue that bicycle lanes be provided on certain streets and byways. Involved parents stand in line to see that children are vaccinated, get their polio shots, and have their chest X rays taken. Of course, all of this takes a considerable amount of time and energy, but this is the only way that accidents and illnesses can be prevented. Concerned parents know where their children are in the afternoons and evenings, even if it means quarrels with pubescent children over parental controls. They spend many hours discussing everything and anything with their children. In the household of the active parent there is very likely more fussing than in homes where no one is present or where an authoritarian silence is maintained. The active parent is aware of the child's achievement in school and becomes informed of his or her potentialities and talents. Thus, anxieties and guilt surrounding a child's achievement can be mollified once the parents are aware of what the problems are. This kind of parenting requires seemingly endless time, energy, and stamina, but the rewards lie in the pleasure of the involvement itself, as well as in the promise of success in the long run.

5. OTHER EMOTIONAL BATTERINGS

In the household of the Battered Parent, pain, depression, and screaming are most common. The first and primary sign of the Battered Parent is that no one in the family seems capable of making any decision—or having a decision stick. Battered parents may try to tell children what to do, but more often, the children's demands come first. Parents may begin by attempting to reason with their child, yet not have the time or energy for such a "rational" approach. Thus, the child hears only half of the parents' instructions—and quickly finds that the rest can be rejected with a scream. Parents yield, and thus each time they put forth any demands, the child will continue to scream. After a while, parents find themselves screaming back. As a result, the child screams more. Usually, the battered parents feel guilty about screaming, which adds to their depression. They may retreat into silence again—whereupon the child may retreat to a corner in silence.

Basically, there is no direction in the family headed by the Battered Parent. Because parental requirements are seldom enforced, there is considerable confusion over who said what or who requires what. Typically, the parent begs the child to perform. The child ignores this request; parent reprimands child; child argues that the parent never made the request clear; parent apologizes. Children in such families come and go as they please, and parents often do not know where they are or what they are up to. Far too often, such permissiveness really is an excuse for *parents* to come and go as they please, without any responsibility—and as a result, their children often feel neglected. Lacking guidance and direction, they make more and more demands on the parents. Even though the parents may be extremely indulgent, giving the child almost everything she or he demands in the way of material goods, the child remains whiny and demanding. Such children often display feelings of discontent, restlessness, and unhappiness. Nothing seems to satisfy them, and without a parent immediately available, they frequently find themselves in trouble. Very often, the chief reason why children wet the bed, disobey, run away, indulge in drugs and alcohol, is to compel a parent to take charge. In order to gain parenting, they intentionally hurt the parent, transferring their pain and depression onto the parent so that it is the parent who suffers. (Children can thus be relieved of any guilt, for according to them, it is their parents' fault that they get in trouble.)

Often, children in such families become major behavior problems at school as well as home, causing the parents additional embarrassment and misery. When the child becomes so out of control, people outside the family usually complain, creating external demands on the parent.

Battered Parents then begin to feel guilty, as if they have not done enough for their children, even though they are in many ways "spoiling" them. They tend to mention their children in terms of despair, apologizing for their behavior with a pained smile. A Battered Parent becomes more and more depressed, feeling guilty and yet not knowing what he or she may be guilty about. The children leave home in the morning unhappy, resentful, and angry, and scream at the teacher. When the teacher finally abandons hope and yells back at the parents (often through school authorities), they then have an excuse to blame the school. The parents also tend to blame others—the neighborhood children, the society at large—but in their own hearts, Battered Parents wonder where *they* went wrong. If the school authorities convince them to go to a child guidance clinic, the child psychiatrist will likely fault the parents, thus adding to their depression.

"WHAT? ME WORRY?"

Although both parent and child may be miserable, most often both will tend to deny that anything at all is wrong. This attitude is often quite puzzling and frustrating to the psychotherapist. Both parent and child are actually quite concerned about their respective misery, of course, but they are quick to blame one another. Hoping to avoid revealing any feelings of guilt, the parent seeking child guidance usually demands that the psychotherapist take over and "cure" the child without involving the parent further. The child recognizes that the parent does feel guilty and thus continues to let the world in general know that his is "a bad parent." However, as long as the parent continues to deny to others as well as to himself or herself that anything is really wrong, they will all continue to suffer.

Since a child learns to express emotions from his or her parents, it behooves them to be most aware of their own feelings. Such awareness *does not* mean that parents must repress their feelings entirely. When they bottle up their emotions, the child is often quite aware that they are holding something back. Usually even the best-controlled parent gives it away by tone of voice, choice of words, stiffness of body or face, gesture or glance—which creates a dilemma. In effect, the child then wonders whether to mimic the emotion or the repression—and more often than not, the child reacts to the emotion. Another source of problems comes when a child tries to act out parents' own repressed emotions and conflicts for them but the child's expression of the denied anger is usually quite subtle and not immediately observable.

For example, Lloyd's father was a prominent member of the police force in their small town. Everybody was aware that Lloyd's father had failed several times to be promoted within the police force. When the City Fathers gathered to select a new police chief, they bypassed Lloyd's father, principally because he was known as a rather passive man, a kindly but not aggressive enforcer of the law. Lloyd, age 11, was an excellent student and most capable athlete, but was often openly combative with other children. His temper flared quickly, sometimes for no apparent reason. He always seemed to be shouting "unfair" and engaging in hot verbal arguments that too frequently ended in fisticuffs. He was frequently disciplined in the classroom and the schoolyard, and despite his athletic prowess he was excluded from the best teams.

When Lloyd entered junior high school, his father was able to get a job as police chief in a slightly larger town nearby—after which Lloyd's behavior changed markedly. He no longer got into fights with other children, but became a model of good sportsmanship.

Mark, Jr., age 13, was quiet and reserved, remarkably like his father in character and looks. A good student, he was well behaved at school and at home. Sharing his father's interest in guns, he frequently went hunting with his father and practiced on the shooting range. Otherwise, he seldom became assertive or aggressive, never pushing himself forward in any social setting.

Shortly after his 14th birthday, he was arrested for shooting at cars on the highway. Five days previously, his mother had left the home with a boyfriend she had been seeing for many months. Her husband had ignored the fact that his wife was flagrantly unfaithful, and after she left, he made no effort to look for her. When Mark asked about her, his father advised Mark not to "let her get under your skin."

In fact, *it is quite common for children to express out loud, or in action the feelings a parent is repressing.* Thus, the child becomes the vehicle for the expression of the parent's feelings. But parents who have successfully repressed their feelings will not realize what the child is doing, and will see only that the child is acting in an unacceptable manner. The parents are likely to be doubly upset, in fact, since the child's expression of their hidden feelings makes it more difficult for the parents to maintain control.

ON DENYING FEELING HURT

As pain increases, most people will do almost anything to avoid it. They butter over their burns, find some soothing salve for their wounds, ask their physicians to give them a shot of morphine or other painkiller. Yet pain serves a normal physiological purpose: It is a natural warning that our body is injured or in danger, and that something should be done about it. If pain were completely nullified, the injury or infection might cripple the person.

The best illustration is a toothache. Very often a person can have good-size cavities destroying the tooth enamel, but if they don't hit the nerve root, then the individual may be unaware of them and take no action. If they are not in constant, severe pain, in fact, many people will avoid the discomfort of going to the dentist and instead allow their teeth to rot away.

Much the same is true of psychological pain, most of which comes in the form of anxiety—also a normal warning signal. This feeling tells us that something may go wrong in our life if we don't watch out. Thus, anxiety, like physiological pain, should drive a person to change her or his behavior in order to avoid being hurt. From time to time, however, almost everyone tries to avoid or ignore the anxiety itself.

Some people have methods of avoiding anxiety altogether. Again, the simplest and most prevalent method of handling the pain is simple denial: "Oh, it doesn't really matter," "It isn't all *that* bad," "I don't *really* feel hurt (or angry, or depressed)." These statements are often belied by a person's behavior: While denying feeling so, they *act* hurt or angry or depressed. Of course, the denial is aimed not only at assuaging and avoiding the hurt, but also at covering feelings that might be socially disapproved. In many cultures, it is not considered adult—especially not manly—to show hurt feelings. Thus, men are much more likely to deny psychological hurts or that something wrong in the family is causing conflicts. However, repressing anxiety usually can be successful for only a short period: Whatever condition is affecting a person's life will not be solved by denial and in fact is likely to grow worse.

As the pain continues and increases, further action *is* usually necessary. Parents who try to deny and repress hurt feelings will be unsuccessful because sooner or later the child will see through their denial and realize that they are not telling the truth. A child who has set out to irritate his parents and make them angry and then finds them saying that they really are not angry at all is likely to increase his efforts to upset them. And the child who is inadvertently irritating his parents certainly will not stop if told that it does not matter. An extreme example to illustrate the point: Mr. O. heard a noise in the loft above the garage. He stepped upstairs to find Paula, his teenage daughter, standing on a chair. A rope with a noose on the end was slung over the rafters. "What are you doing?" he asked.

"Nothing, father," she replied.

"Well, then," said Mr. O., "come down to dinner." Of course, his attempt to ignore his daughter's obvious suicide attempt was actually harmful. Paula continued to make suicide attempts until she was caught by a school authority and put into the hospital. (For a complete analysis of this case, see my casebook *The Experience of Anxiety.*)

A somewhat more complex and extensive method of handling anxiety is what psychologists call *reaction formation,* in which a person becomes involved in some other behavior in the hopes of avoiding pain.

For example, people who find it very painful and difficult to express anger may instead attempt to set up their life to avoid situations in which anger might arise. Such people might try to be so extremely well-behaved that no one could ever criticize them. They may become perfectionists or try to be outstanding successes so that no one will ever be angry at them. They may also develop counterreactions such as being extra cheerful, always smiling and pleasant, and thus never arouse any anger in anyone else (and in fact, make anyone who might be angry at them feel guilty).

Again, this does not include changing behavior so as to *resolve* the conflict. Rather, reaction formations are still another method of merely avoiding pain or anxiety without making those changes necessary to solve the problem. But when a person finds successful ways to avoid being hurt, he or she is likely to use them over and over again. Reaction formations *are* likely to be more successful methods of avoiding anxiety, and thus become set habit patterns that then become part of one's character—so that neither the individual nor others know the very extreme ways the person has of avoiding such pain.

In dealing with children, reaction formations are also a bit more successful than simple denial. The sticky-sweet, constantly ever-loving parent is much harder for the child to defy. A good example is in Ingmar Bergman's movie *Face to Face*, where the ever-loving grandmother would punish the fearful girl by making her stay in a dark closet. Yet there was never a harsh word from the grandmother. In fact, as long as the girl behaved perfectly, she was given rewards. On the other hand, the grandmother never fully recognized the child's mixed feelings of grief and anger over her parents' death. Instead, she reacted by seeing the child as ungrateful for all the wonderful things she supplied.

Parents who are using reaction formation may even admit to some hurt feelings, but never see themselves involved in creating the situation at all. Thus, when a child screams, "I hate you, I hate you," perfectionistic parents who demand high standards of behavior from the child may be astounded and make a great pretense of having hurt feelings. Even at such moments, however, such parents would likely deny that they were really angry.

As might be imagined, such a parental reaction formation can drive a child to even more extreme behavior. As a result the child is perceived as evil, constantly defying the good parent who doesn't deserve such a reaction. The tragedy becomes even deeper because such children are quite unsatisfactory and there are no rewards for the parent. In the long run, parents feel justified in their anger because they have done everything that they should for the child and have always been perfect parents, only to be treated with such ingratitude. Often their children (especially adolescents) go out of their way to commit outrageous violations of parental standards just to see if the parents will ever be honest enough in their feelings to get truly angry.

A most extreme form of dealing with hurt feelings and anxiety is one that psychologists label "projection." Actually projection is a method of dealing with blame and guilt, but this type of defense is commonly used to handle general anxiety as well. Projection is best exemplified in the Biblical parable of seeing the mote in one's neighbor's eye. Projection not only denies anxiety, but pretends that it is the *other* person who is hurt and anxious. Worried and anxious parents say to the child, "Oh, you poor dear, you must feel dreadful," projecting their own anxieties onto the child.

Such projection is very common in the overprotective parent; parents who go to extremes to make sure that a child is not hurt or in any danger are really projecting their own worries. When a child is overdressed against the cold or rain and is not allowed to go places where she or he might be hurt or come under the influence of "bad company," it is the parent and not the child who is avoiding anxiety. The evil is thus usually seen in the environment, rather than in any behavior by either parent or child. Parents who are trying to squelch antisocial impulses in their child quite often use the excuse that the child is in danger from some outside influence, and take extra steps to avoid having the child influenced by his peers. If the child is failing at school, it's the school's fault. If the child is ill, it is because the doctor has not done the right thing. If a child is in trouble with the law, it is because the child has been influenced by delinquent peers—or, alternatively, the alleged delinquency is no crime at all, but the reaction of overzealous and prejudiced police. These factors may actually contribute to the child's difficulties, but the point is that too many parents project their feelings of guilt and uneasiness onto the community, using social ills as scapegoats for their own responsibility.

HURTING BACK

One of the most natural reactions to being hurt is to hurt back, to seek revenge. Unfortunately, parents and children often get involved in round after round of "hurting back." Such rounds of revenge are even more common between siblings. Very often, it begins when a parent draws up a list of accusations against the child, as if the parent were a prosecutor. Faced with these accusations, the child then draws up his own list of the parent's failings. The parent then sets up punishments to fit the crimes; the child in turn rejects the punishments and sets up demands to prove that his parents are bad parents. In essence, the child's argument is "Why should I obey you if you don't love me?" The humiliated parents say, "Why should we love you if you don't obey us?" Another version of this same vicious circle of hurting back is the child's accusation, "You never trust me"—to which the parent responds, "You can't be trusted." Both sides are really shouting "Prove it!" And neither side, of course, will accept any kind of proof.

Hurts get magnified until a wall of hostility is built up that seems impossible to overcome. And far too often this circle of accusation and retort develops into a series of revengeful acts.

This pattern of revenge is illustrated by Douglas N., who constantly snarled at his parents, making vague threats against them and disregarding any of their commands. When they complained that he never bathed and that his room was a filthy shambles, he retorted that they had refused to buy him any paint to paint his room or buy him any new clothes. Mrs. N. threatened that she wouldn't buy him any new clothes until he brought the ones he had to the laundry to be washed, and she refused to enter his room because it smelled. Likewise, his father argued that he wouldn't spend any money on Douglas because Douglas didn't take care of his things.

Douglas retorted that his parents constantly favored his younger sister, who always acted like an angel. His parents then would respond that Susie never gave them any trouble and that if he would only obey, he would get the same treatment. Douglas would then attack Susie with both words and fists and, of course, get punished by his parents—whereupon he would threaten Susie further, blaming her for his difficulties.

Douglas would come home from school hungry and help himself to food in the refrigerator; Mrs. N. would then complain that he was extending her food budget; Douglas would retort that she never bought any decent food and was starving him. Douglas would take his bus money, buy snacks with it, and hitchhike to school. His parents then would not give him the money, and Douglas would refuse to drive to school with them. When Mr. N. punished Douglas by restricting his allowance, Douglas would steal money from his mother's purse, claiming that he deserved it.

The pattern is classic: Parent attempts to limit, control, and punish; child reacts by rebelling and defying. Each in turn feels justified and is "trying to teach the child (or parent) a lesson." I have known children actually to admit they were failing in school in order to "get my mother off my back." In some way, the children seemed to believe that if they were utter failures, their parents would give up. The same pattern of behavior is seen in the judge who metes out more severe sentences each time a delinquent boy defies the law, then is puzzled when the youngster becomes more bitter and angry at society.

ON SAYING "OUCH"

When parents get extremely defensive, or when parents and children set up circles of revenge, it is often difficult to get them to alter their behavior. It would be far easier if parents and children could learn to handle their feelings of hurt and anxiety more directly in the first place. These defenses and revenge cycles could be dispensed with altogether if people could develop the habit of recognizing anxiety—and enduring it at least long enough to see if they can solve the underlying conflict.

Of course it takes considerable strength of character to endure physiological or psychological pain; it is much easier to rush to the medicine cabinet for some Valium or other painkiller. The ability to say to oneself, "Hey, something's wrong and I'd better do something about it," requires a level of maturity and inner strength that many adults—let alone children—do not possess.

Psychotherapy consists largely of assisting people to build up that strength so that they are able to say, "Ouch" to themselves. Although the term "hurt feelings" may be clear enough in itself, it may actually have several different implications:

° *Being rejected:* One reaches out a hand to someone and finds no return gesture of friendliness or affection. Hurt feelings are, in a sense, unrequited love. Children hurt parents' feelings when they do not return the affection, support, and trust their parents give them.

° *Disappointment:* A parent has expectations for the child; if the child fails, the parental pride is hurt. In this sense of hurt feelings, the parent receives no satisfaction from the child. The Yiddish word *naches* sums up this parental pride; the parent who gets no "naches" is hurt, feeling deprived of the reward for all the efforts she or he has put out in being a parent.

° *Being insulted and degraded:* It is not merely parental love that is rejected; the child rejects the parent as a person. A child may consider his parents old-fashioned or unfeeling, without understanding, cruel or unthinking. She or he regards the best efforts of sincere devoted parents as really injurious, overrestricting, limiting, even obnoxious. He or she challenges the parents' best intentions, calls them selfish, and alleges that they seek only to control and ruin his life. Although parents may know that such allegations are false and merely the reactions of an angry child, they hurt nevertheless.

By saying "ouch," a parent recognizes and admits to feeling pain. One is then able to look to see what is hurting, what needs to be done in the case of psychological pain, what changes in behavior may be necessary. *Recognizing the hurt is thus the first major step toward its resolution.*

Sometimes this is all that is necessary. The parent who expresses feelings of hurt and anxiety in an open, honest fashion is likely to gain the child's sympathetic attention. Moreover, the parent who can make such expressions of feeling is likely to find that children will in turn let the parent know their feelings. Most individuals, especially children, do not like to hurt other people, but if a person does not tell others that his feelings are hurt, he may be trampled on even more. Thus, you need to say to your child, "I get anxious when you do that." Or, "you know that you have hurt my feelings." Any such statements will make most children stop and think about their behavior.

Such statements also will help the parent. If a mother finds that her feelings are hurt because of her children's expectations, they may alter their demands. Inversely, if parents find that they have hurt their child's pride, then they may change *their* expectations. Once such facts are stated openly, it is possible to alter either the child's behavior or the parents'. They may be able to say to themselves, "Yes, we would hope for more from our child, but maybe that hope isn't realistic." Or either parent can say, "I would love to have my children closer to me, but I know that they must become more independent." Thus, parents admit the present hurt, but may be able to change their behavior so as to feel less hurt in the future.

6. THE MONSTER AND THE HERO

Resistance to parental direction appears in children's behavior at almost every stage of development. But real bullheaded obstinacy is most characteristic of these middle years of childhood—ages 6 to 12. Most children during this period also have their sweet side and can be quite compliant at times, but the "No" in them is usually stronger now even than it was at age two when they first began to use the word. These years display a contrary "willfulness," as our Puritan ancestors used to term it, rather than the open rebellious independence of adolescence.

Actually the negative edge present in every child of this age is merely one aspect of the normal development of middle childhood, or what Freud termed the latency years.

This negativism is merely part of the latency child's "task," which is to develop self-control: the main emotional and social goal for latency-age children—and for their parents.

The fairy tales and legends of nearly every country throughout history have two central figures: the devil, monster, dragon, giant, or witch, who has to be subdued by a magical hero, Superman, a knight in shining armor, or Jack the Giant Killer. In the 20th century, these monsters and heroes have not disappeared but have been made more realistic and prevalent in children's cartoons on television. Although the modern cartoon puts a humorous spoof on both dragon and hero to a certain extent, the underlying message remains the same: there is monstrous danger to be overcome, and a hero—very often a youth—is called on to conquer that danger. In modern TV Land, one of the all-powerful comic heroes is Mighty Mouse, who typifies the power of the little person to conquer everything.

It does not take much adult imagination or insight to realize that the monster to be conquered lies within. As the cartoon figure Pogo says wisely, "We have met the enemy and he is us." The enemy is constituted of those unacceptable impulses that the latency child must suppress and control. The monster and the hero are thus two opposing sides in the development of what the psychoanalysts call the superego, more popularly known as the conscience.

Actually, superego development begins much earlier in childhood. Preschool children tell their teddy bear, "No, no, no," and spank it; they know a great deal of what is right or wrong. The major difference between the preschooler and the latency child is that the preschooler has not yet developed any "internalized" self-controls. By and large, preschoolers behave because they fear parental authority.

Children under the age of six have a stop-and-go conscience. As long as the signal light is turned on, they will obey because they do not wish to offend. But if no parental signal is immediately available, they may proceed without deep feelings of guilt. Small children may be ashamed at times, but do not commonly experience the adult feeling of guilt.

They cry because they know Mommy will spank them, not because they have done wrong. Around age five to six, however, the child begins to evaluate acts as having a moral value: right or wrong. A child's moral values are, of course, modeled largely after those of parents or other authorities. Children at this age often quote their parents, with "My mommy says," or "My daddy says" becoming common phrases in their language. They soon are saying, "The teacher says," as well. This modeling procedure is of major interest to many students of developmental psychology, but psychologists are not yet sure why most youngsters begin to develop an internal conscience at about this age. Very likely, the child may be motivated to behave *like* the parental model because it is necessary for him to leave home and enter school *without* the parent present.

Freud maintained that the development of the superego was consequent to the resolution of what he described as the Oedipal complex. According to Freud, the child at this age gives up the popular fantasy of violating the incest taboo and instead models himself or herself upon the parent of the same sex. The little boy now no longer fears his father's retaliation because of their rivalry for his mother's affection. Rather, he begins to behave in an almost super-masculine fashion. Classical psychoanalytic theory also contends that little girls develop a conscience by relinquishing their role as "daddy's little girl" and modeling themselves on their mothers. There is probably more than a grain of truth in these assumptions; the evidence is becoming increasingly obvious that children do have sexual interests in early childhood. Today, only the most prudish of psychologists denies the fact, even though some of the Freudian theses about infant sexuality probably bear some revision.

Infants show physiological signs of sexuality. Little boys have erections, and little girls are easily stimulated by any pressure on their genitals. In both sexes, open masturbation in infancy is quite common. As yet, of course, the child is not physiologically or socially able to enter any kind of sexual relationship.

And so, soon after kindergarten, where children often have "sweethearts," boys and girls turn their backs on each other and the sexes maintain a separation. In these latency years, little boys "hate" girls and avoid contact with them, just as the little girls consider the boys "monsters" and have nothing to do with them. This excessive rejection of sexuality is the children's way of handling something which they would otherwise find impossible to deal with. At this point, the important thing is that the latency-age child begins to struggle with the monster inside and do the Super-Hero job of controlling it.

The monstrous feelings inside the child are multiple. The sexual monster is a bother only when overstimulation occurs. To Mighty Mouse, however, the monster of aggression is often a far greater threat. Angry and destructive feelings are far more frequently present for the child and frequently an equal threat to parents.

All of literature, beginning with the Biblical tale of Cain and Abel, illustrates that in the heart of the most innocent babe lies murder. Children's preoccupation with violence and killing did not begin with the advent of television (although I do feel that television has made violence too realistic for children to countenance). If allowed, preschool children will commit acts of violence on other children, animals, and themselves. Fortunately, they don't have the physical strength or know-how to be truly murderous, but they often openly express homicidal feelings and need to be reassured by their parents that Mother and Father will not *permit* them to commit such acts of violence. Small children may stomp their feet and scream, "I'll kill you, I'll kill you," but their firm intentions are usually short-lived. Children who begin to throw things, kick, and be destructive are usually short-circuited by the parent or teacher who (at least) isolates them until they cool down.

Usually, parents with a newborn child control the preschooler in a preventive fashion by giving equal attention to both children and thus dampening the rivalry. The wise parent praises the child for being bigger, more responsible, more independent—and thus superior to the new baby. The latency-age child is much less likely to overtly express anger, however. When a new baby arrives, the older child may not feel quite so displaced or rejected, and not quite so murderous.

Any violent feelings children may display toward parents or other authorities are usually assuaged, too, if whatever discipline and controls an adult places on them are equally balanced by affection, praise, and rewards. Open screams of murderous anger are less likely, but latency-age children may look very angry and demonstrate by marching off or otherwise avoiding contact with those against whom they have a grudge—and, of course, they get into frequent fights with their siblings or other peers.

In short, the latency-age child's control over aggression is much less complete than his repression of sexuality. However, latency-age children are much more likely to appeal to authority to intervene and pass judgment on their enemies. They raise complaints to their parents about their playmates' or siblings' "unfair" behavior. There is less open fisticuffs, and far more name-calling. An older sister can drive her little brother into beating upon her—whereupon she wins, because *he* has acted like the baby and lost control, while she is Miss Innocent Angel.

The quick jab of the elbow or furtive kick is more likely to occur than a rain of blows, though a checker game between two eight-year-olds can result in tears and blood because one or more participants will try to fudge when they think they're losing. In the playground of the average elementary school during recess, the children spend much more time arguing over the rules of a game than they do actually playing it. Charges of "No fair," and "You're cheating," ring through the air. Regulations at school and at home are met with supersophisticated arguments that make the weary teacher and parent wonder if the child is going to grow up to be an attorney. Latency-age children seem to want everything precise and exact. Woe betide the parent who drives thirty-two miles an hour through a thirty-mile zone with a critical nine-year-old in the back seat. Often meals have to be cooked "just right" and only certain foods are acceptable. (Wearing the right clothes is more of an adolescent obsession.)

Within the latency child these internal conflicts are often manifested in ordinary but pervasive childhood fears. Children are afraid of the dark not because they really believe in monsters, but because their aggressive and sexual impulses are more likely to appear vividly and intensely in their dreams. They frequently develop other little phobias, usually transitory but related to the "monsters" within. Quite often, what the child actually fears is retaliation from those whom he *would* murder or from those who would be offended should he express sexual feelings. These fears also act as brakes on the child's sensual and aggressive impulses. The wise parent, of course, accepts heroes and the monster as a normal part of childhood. Most parents probably do not quite realize that these legends do refer to the development of the child's conscience, but they do, by their actions, reinforce and support the inner policeman, the good guy, the self-controlling child.

Earlier in life, children behave themselves largely because they fear parental disapproval or punishment. Even during the latency years, of course, the child may avoid disapproved behavior because "My mother will murder me." However, the major difference is that the infant behaves because the mother is there to make him obey. When the mother is not there, the younger child easily yields to temptation. Gradually the parent's words sink into the child's mind and he or she starts to behave as if they were being repeated in her or his head as on a tape cassette. And the super-hero usually prevents the villain from committing any act of murder; the idealized policeman within usually catches the criminal before the crime is committed.

The child's sexuality at this age is a strange phenomenon: At one and the same time the child may seem completely oblivious to the sensual implications in his environment and yet be excessively modest and easily embarrassed. If children of this age do become aware of even a hint of something sexual—such as the hero kissing the heroine in the cowboy movie—they are likely to squirm with embarrassment. They are very sensitive to family and community morals, and thus the parental model presented to children is very important. However, the standards regarding sexuality aggression are in flux, creating conflicts for both parents and children. Far too often children are sexually overstimulated, and when they have to struggle with double standards the parents usually become battered. Where there are sexual conflicts within a family, they may be reflected in the latency-age child's behavior. In children of this age, the most common reflections of a family sexual conflict are either a bashful social withdrawal or the entire opposite—hyperactivity.

For example, Michael, age 8 and in the third grade, was always on his feet in the classroom. He seemed to have considerable difficulty in concentrating and sitting still. He wriggled about all the time and seemed anxious to talk, but had little to say. When faced with his behavior, he was apologetic and promised to be good, but was out of his seat the next moment. Michael frequently quarreled with other children and tried to dominate them, but at the same time he seemed desperately eager to make friends and pursued other children to get them to play with him. The teacher noticed that he often seemed to have his hand on his genitals and asked to be allowed to go to the bathroom in the middle of class.

An interview by the school psychologist revealed that Michael lived with his mother and his sister, a year younger, in a single-bedroom apartment. Michael's mother was a young woman, scarcely twenty-five, but quite obese. She was openly affectionate with both children, often hugging and kissing them. When she tried to be affectionate with Michael he withdrew with noticeable embarrassment. Recently she had separated from her husband, who went off to live with another woman. She was trying to get by on a pittance from the welfare office. Her husband contributed no money, yet he would drop by periodically; either there would be a huge fight or she would attempt to entice him back into the home by having sex with him. The house was poorly furnished, and the walls very thin. Michael's mother said that when they were quarreling or making love, she often tried to keep her husband quiet so that he would not wake the children in the next room. She admitted that she usually slept with the two children but was immediately apologetic, explaining that they only had one warm blanket and hastily adding that when she slept with the children, she always wore her underwear.

Shortly thereafter, Michael's mother found a boy-friend who supported them financially and who later moved in as husband and father. Thereupon, Michael's behavior at school ameliorated considerably.

Hyperactivity is the most common reaction to sexual stimulation in boys—although it is by no means the only reaction; nor does all hyperactivity in boys result from sexual conflicts in the family. Because a high level of physical activity is the norm at this age, however, it is natural that the release of energy would be the symptom to be exaggerated when conflict occurs.

Although girls may also react to stress (particularly sexual stimulation) by hyperactivity, our society frowns on such aggressive feminine behavior and instead countenances and even supports passive withdrawal. Thus, it is far more common for girls to react to sensual stress by becoming excessively bashful and silent.

For example, Shirley, age 8, seemed almost unable to recite in the classroom. When called upon, she would stand up and turn pink and begin to wring her hands, grabbing at the edge of her skirt and winding it up in her hands to reveal her underwear. If this was drawn to her attention, she would become even more upset. Even when spoken to in a kindly fashion, she might burst into tears or run from the classroom. Her written work was **always** excellent, however, and she seemed to be absorbing her lessons without difficulty. The teacher noted that Shirley seemed overly withdrawn on the playground as well. At most, she would participate in formal, structured play led by the teacher. But when free play was allowed during recess or lunch, she often sat on the bench by herself, staring off into space.

During the usual teacher-parent conference, her parents denied that they saw anything wrong with the child at home and declared that they believed her to be perfectly happy. Within a month or so thereafter, however, Shirley did seem to be ill and refused to come to school. Medical examination revealed no physical illness, but she complained of being weak and unable to leave home. At this point the family was referred to the school psychologist. Again, they declared that Shirley was normally a very happy child and they could think of no stress at home that might be disturbing her. They felt that perhaps the teacher had overexaggerated Shirley's behavior at school, which had so embarrassed her that she did not wish to attend.

In further discussion, they admitted that they had considerably more problems with their impudent and rebellious 15-year-old daughter, Marie, who had run away from home several times. They neglected to tell the psychologist that Marie had had an abortion, but this was in the family's medical records at the hospital. When the psychologist advised the family that he knew of Marie's abortion, the parents admitted that they had had trouble for several years with Marie's aggressive behavior and sexual acting-out. In fact, the mother admitted, perhaps she had neglected Shirley somewhat because so much concern and attention was directed toward Marie.

During this family discussion of Marie's problems, Shirley was most uncomfortable and finally ran from the room weeping. In a private interview, Shirley admitted that Marie's behavior embarrassed her considerably. On the other hand, she regarded her parents as very harsh with Marie, and felt a great deal of sympathy toward her older sister, with whom she seemed to be identifying. The psychologist felt that the family's concern with Marie's sexuality had upset Shirley's attempts to deny her own sexual urges, as would have been normal at her age.

Less common but far more socially disturbing was Lisa's reaction. This 9-year-old girl complained to her mother that an elderly neighbor had sexually molested her. The mother, very upset, called the police. The man confessed that he had allowed the child to see him naked with an erect penis, but denied that he had touched her in any way. He was extremely disturbed and apologetic, but said that the child had been in and out of his home quite frequently, almost without his or his wife's permission.

As the psychologist the court had assigned to this case, I interviewed both the offender and his alleged victim. The man admitted that he was quite sexually frustrated since for well over a year, his wife had been quite ill and thus was unable to have intercourse. He and his wife reported that Lisa had been in their home quite frequently over the past several months. They liked the child and welcomed her, since they had no grandchildren. She was affectionate and seemed particularly attracted to the man in question, often sitting on his lap and showering him with kisses. She ate many meals with them, always saying that her mother was not at home. Several times, the wife had tried to contact the mother and had, indeed, found no one there. However, once or twice when they had insisted Lisa return home, she had burst into tears. They had taken her home and found lights on in the house, but no parent present.

When interviewed, Lisa admitted that the man in question had never actually touched her but claimed that he had encouraged her to look at him and touch him. Her story varied, however, and every time she told it she seemed to be telling a different version. She was very excited and seemed to regard the whole business as an adventure. In discussing the situation with the psychologist, she revealed that she knew quite a bit about sexual facts and was very excited by them.

At this point, I was able to meet with Lisa's mother, a very depressed woman who started off her discussion of Lisa's problem by remarking, "Here's just another thing that adds to my burdens of life." She explained that she had been quite ill from time to time and regretted that she had not always been able to watch over Lisa. She made frequent trips to the doctor but agreed that her illness was not very well diagnosed, and that perhaps she was primarily depressed. She said that she had appreciated the fact that these neighbors had welcomed Lisa to their home and watched after her, and she felt badly that she had not made contacts with them. Asked about her other problems, she explained that she was very angry at her husband, who had recently forsaken her for another woman.

When asked about this, Lisa admitted that she frequently spent weekends with her father and his girl friend in their single-room apartment, and volunteered that she had observed them engaged in sexual relations. I believed that Lisa, overstimulated sexually by the father's behavior, felt unable to be in touch with her mother's withdrawal and depression. The court decided to accept the elderly neighbor's reduced plea to "disturbing the peace," and he was put on probation. The court also directed that Lisa and her mother enter into psychotherapy.

Such overt interest in sex is of course very rare in children of this age, and when such overt sexual involvements do occur they almost always are the result of extrasexual stimulation—at least in my experience. However, it is doubtful that self-stimulation disappears altogether in latency years, although the intense psychological repression of sexuality may cause a temporary lull in the actual physiological impulse. In any case, the latency child who publicly seems oblivious to and easily embarrassed by sexuality often has considerable secret sexual curiosity. Children of this age love dirty words, even though they do not seem really aware of their meaning. For example, my grandson, who was learning to read, remarked with a teasing look that he knew a word that began with *F*. "Ho, Ho," I replied. "Just what is the word that you know that begins with *F*?"

"Well," he said wisely, "it's *F* for vagina!" Thus, while struggling valiantly to be a sexless Superman or Wonder Woman, the latency child picks up gutter words with intense curiosity.

Parents are often unaware that the children are being so stimulated; most of all, parents ignore the fact that sexual stimulation is prevalent through Western society. Almost every advertisement tries to sell its product by stimulating or titillating the users. Children who spend hours in front of the television see these ads continuously, as well as those in magazines, newspapers, and billboards. Open references to sexuality also appear in adult conversations much more frequently than ever before. This is not to say that sexuality need be made a hush-hush matter as it was in Victorian days, or that parents should not inform children about sex *as their curiosity arises.*

But parents should be aware that constant conflict exists within the latency child between Mighty Mouse and the devouring cat of sexuality. When children are inadvertently exposed to sexual stimulation in the movies, on television, or in public conversation, they may need some support and explanation from their mothers and fathers.

Any parent aware that children have been so stimulated should discuss the situation and tell them there's no need to be concerned about these things. In fact, it is a good idea for parents to let children know from time to time that there is no need for them to act in *any* sexual fashion, and that no demands will be made upon them.

For example, when a son maintains that he hates girls or a daughter that she hates boys, support this denial of sexuality so as to help him or her deal with the stimulation— for which there *is* no good answer at this age. Similarly, when embarrassed children remark that they regard the lovemaking in a movie as silly or even repugnant, again support their feelings: Agree that it's perfectly normal to regard such behavior as silly when one is 8 or 9 years old. Don't add "Later you will appreciate it," but merely leave it that the child need not accept such sexual stimulation at all, even when it is a perfectly normal excitement for the adult or teenager.

If our society has become far more lax in the control of our sexual impulses, there has not really been any relaxation regarding aggression. Perhaps some parents have learned to tolerate children's open expression of aggression a bit more, but by and large I doubt there has been much change regarding aggressive behavior in our society.

Before discussing self-control over aggressive impulses, it may help to define some terms. *Aggression* refers primarily to that very natural and normal push to get what one wants without depending on anyone else. Aggressive behavior need not be violent at all, nor need it entail any kind of anger. In Western society, in fact, normal aggressive behavior that fosters competition is usually highly approved of. The main problem arises when one person's needs—and aggressive behavior in meeting those needs—conflict with someone *else's* needs and aggressive behavior. Thus, if two children seek the same satisfaction at the same moment, there is bound to be some clash and conflict. Such conflict may well involve anger, even violence.

However, there is also a type of behavior psychologists call "passive-aggressive," in which a person in effect forces others to do what he wants merely by not doing *anything*. Such passive aggression is, of course, typified by Mahatma Gandhi's nonviolent disobedience; the British were forced finally to give in to Gandhi and his followers, piece by piece, until India was set free. Such behavior is quite common in children, who resist by noncompliance. Sometimes, however, it is difficult to distinguish between such behavior and utter dependence. For the purposes of this book, *aggressiveness* means something more independent and overt.

Again, anger is not the same thing as being aggressive; it is, rather, a feeling that people communicate to one another when they feel in danger of being hurt. When animals feel threatened, they growl. The hair rises on the backs of their necks, their eyes narrow, and their claws raise—and very often, such expression of anger will actually *prevent* a fight. Take the common situation in which one dog invades another's territory. The invader may not even know that he is trespassing until he hears the growls of the possessive animal.

In human behavior, similarly, anger is often a necessary communication. Without it, people might not know that they have insulted, hurt the feelings of, or otherwise threatened a fellow human being. Usually, it is enough for one person to say, "Watch out! I feel very angry when you do that, and if you persist, I intend to take some sort of action about it." Like any other animal, humans will also back off in such instances unless, of course, they intend fully to become involved in a struggle. Situations become crucial when anger and aggression are combined and the individual threatens to become violent and destructive. Because of this danger, most societies have ways in which disputes can be settled without violence. The more "primitive" societies even have very formal ways in which anger can be expressed, such as in dances or ritual ceremonies.

Sometimes conflict of interests can be handled quite peacefully. At other times, loud arguments and screaming do occur, but actual physical combat is highly discouraged.

For a Western child, learning how to handle aggressive impulses and anger becomes very difficult because, in what are called the "civilized" societies, anger is usually muted and the social rules for settling conflicts are complex at best, and often very vague. Western society promotes and praises aggressive competition, and the prohibition against individual violence is never clear-cut.

Open violence was, of course, countenanced in the so-called lawless West, but a good example of it on the 19th century schoolground is seen in the novel *The Hoosier Schoolmaster*, published before 1850. Children play cruel and violent tricks on the schoolteacher, who in turn beats them unmercifully for the slightest violations in the classroom. At that time, such exchange of violence between child and teacher was the accepted form. (Even today, there is public discussion as to whether teachers should be allowed to impose physical punishment upon children.) Many of our legends, plays, and stories still depict individual violence as heroic. The child sees violence on TV and in the movies, in fairy tales and in the Bible. Nearly all religions have a rule such as "Thou shalt not kill." Of course, such a commandment is entirely disregarded in times of war. At least until the Vietnam War, war heroes were highly praised and publicly encouraged. Even today there is considerable disagreement as to whether the American public might support further wars; often killing and other violence is justified by law, as in capital punishment and self-defense.

Children attempting to handle normal aggression and anger are well aware of these discrepancies in our moral values because they are so well portrayed in fiction and in nonfiction, in the press, and on television. They are told repeatedly that they must not express their anger in physical violence, but the language of violence is very common in public schoolgrounds, and in far too many urban schools, unfortunately. Open acts of violence between children do take place; it is most obvious in interracial conflicts. Moreover, there are different standards regarding sexual and aggressive behavior for each sex. These "sexist" values are also important determinants in the child's moral development. But, because these double-standard traditions have no basis in reality and are often inconsistent, both children and parents become confused as to what is proper and what is wrong.

There is a constant disparity between what is said and what occurs. And the inconsistency continues to increase. On the one hand, there is a greater move toward brotherhood, more emphasis on tolerance as a way of existence between individuals, and a greater insistence on rational approaches to solving human conflict. At the same time, professional psychologists and society in general insist on more open expressions of anger. The use of angry words and obscene language is actually promoted. As has been discussed previously, it *is* necessary to let other people know about our feelings. But since children often equate words with action, it is difficult for a child to discriminate between the healthy expression of anger and the use of violence.

It is in this area of aggression-control that parents most often become battered—not so much by the child as by the society in which the family lives. Thus, in a society that preaches nonviolence and practices violence, parents have a most difficult time in guiding a child to learn control over aggressive impulses, where standards of behavior and morals are most variable and shifting.

But the job is not impossible!

7. HELPING YOUR CHILD LEARN SELF-CONTROL

Erik Erikson's book *Childhood and Society* describes in detail the various ways in which children learn self-control. Children seem to have an almost biological drive to develop these self-controls, and it is amazing how often they are developed with little or no assists from parents. Still, child rearing demands considerable time and energy. The parent who sits back, hoping that by some kind of miracle children will rear themselves, is likely to end up in trouble. The passive approach to child rearing also results in the parents' own victimization, for children—who demand some sort of discipline and guidance—will become outrageous and uncontrolled if they receive little attention.

The abilities to think for oneself and control one's impulses, developed during the latency years, do not merely blossom from the inside; rather, they are created by the interaction between the child's natural maturation and the environmental limitations and encouragement that are placed on the child. In the long run, parents obtain the kind of children they expect and create. Whether children become passively submissive and secretly hostile people, or develop into independent, self-guided individuals depends a great deal upon the type of discipline you use.

If parents want a completely docile, passive child, they should use authoritarian methods of child rearing that result in immediate and complete compliance. Such a child learns to fear the punishment that will result from even slight infractions. However, though children disciplined chiefly by punishment learn the lessons very quickly, they really never accept good behavior as their *own*. Instead, such children view the lesson as something external to themselves, which they hate. Obedience from such children may be instant, but is grudging, and they wait for the time that they can slip away from parental authority.

Fear of punishment also often results in stored-up anger that usually comes out later in life, in direct or indirect fashion. Such children may also become adults who obey orders, constantly needing some guidance and rules from the society about them and becoming uneasy when they have to make decisions on their own.

On the other hand, children who are praised for their acceptable (or effective) behavior, whose lapses are treated as temporary "goofs" rather than as "sins," are admittedly more willful. A democratic parent expects the child to obey without continued admonishment, and thus rears a self-controlled-and-self-guided individual. In fact, children who are praised for the behavior parents want to instill become proud of themselves. Such children do accept parental standards as their own and, when they falter, feel genuinely guilty rather than merely ashamed and angry.

Most parents do not really understand the use of rewards as discipline. Too many parents hand out rewards almost automatically, without requiring that they be earned— usually because American parents do not place very heavy requirements on preschool children. There is an old saying that children do not deserve love, but *need* it. This saying is only partly true, however, and becomes less and less so as the child grows older. A parent should never deprive a child of basic affection as a matter of punishment; what is needed instead is to give privileges that the child must earn.

For example, preschool children may have a set bedtime. No matter what the TV program at that hour may be, they are not permitted to watch it. Parents may choose to expand the children's evening hours, but this expansion need not come automatically. They should be allowed to watch another half hour of TV not merely because they are older, but because they've assumed a definite piece of self-responsibility and continue to perform in the expected fashion. Similarly, parents should not grant an automatic allowance, but should find some way for children to earn money (over and above what they might need for lunch or carfare).

Most important is that a child earn special privileges or special gifts. In fact, it is often a good idea to set up special rewards for required performance. Loving parents are continuously alert to their child's feelings, difficulties, and successes. If the child fails to meet parental expectations, they don't necessarily withhold, but rather say, in effect, "Dear, it's too bad you didn't make it, but try better next time." Do not give a child the reward if he or she does not succeed in performing the task, but be careful not to set tasks beyond the child's abilities. Recognize that the child is not able to achieve, but also recognize that she or he is not yet ready for the reward. If necessary, assign some simpler task with a lesser reward so as to avoid complete disappointment.

Parents who use rewards systematically often find they seldom have to "punish" their children—particularly when the reward is social approval and affection. A child does not need to be bribed with cash, or win a prize, or even be given very special privileges. Usually, it is quite sufficient to say, "I'm very proud of you," or "I really love you extra when you do that," or "I appreciate it," or "I enjoyed our day together because you did such-and-such." A pat on the head, a hug, a kiss, are the greatest rewards a child can receive, and are the ones that most children treasure the most. Yet many parents forget to give these very simple rewards—or fear that they are insufficient.

If you make it clear to children how delighted you are that they have behaved themselves, Mighty Mouse will prevail. In fact, even if you do little or nothing but merely permit a child to work out the resolution of these conflicts, it is likely that Mighty Mouse will win. But even parents who basically trust their children's ability to behave in public too often forget to praise them and support them when they've been through some trial or temptation. Away from home, children may find it difficult to avoid joining in some activity that they know parents would consider naughty. Thus, when children report to the parent on the naughtiness of other children, they're often in effect saying, "You can have confidence in me." The overly anxious parent who does not trust the child also becomes battered. It is extremely important to tell children how proud you are that they did not join in the naughtiness. Such praise won't necessarily encourage them to be tattletales; rather, it will support them in the development of their own social consciences.

Again, it must be emphasized that when a parent praises children for good behavior and "models" such behavior for them consistently, it is most likely that the children will copy. For example, if parents consistently say "Please" and "Thank you" and praise children for doing the same, the phrases will automatically ring in their heads. At times, especially in these latency years, you may despair because of your child's many lapses in saying "Please" and "Thank you," but it is often amazing how friends and neighbors (and especially in-laws) will tell you what a polite and well-behaved child you have, much to your amazement—and, of course, to your pleasure. Such social politeness is only one such lesson you hope your child will learn from you. Of course, this absorption of parental dictates occurs because children *do* identify with their parents, an identification process that usually takes place most easily and most intensely when the child has a great deal of affection and respect for the parent.

The main reason why parents don't hand out affection for the behavior they want is that they themselves have likely been reared by far more traditional methods. Parents who were punished as children usually expect that they should punish in order to make their own offspring behave. While parents harbor old resentments at their own punitive parents which they never could express, they are shocked and angered when their own children are openly defiant or rude, because these resentments are reawakened.

It should be noted that corporal punishment is not always a part of the traditional approach. In India and other parts of Asia, parents who strike their children are considered criminals. But ancestor worship remains prevalent in such ancient cultures, and the willful or disobedient child is made to feel intensely guilty. For example, Erik Erikson contends that Gandhi's nonviolent approach to politics originated in his guilt over his disrespect to his own father. The systematic use of rewards given in a gentle but firm fashion is effective with most children—most of the time. Children who learn that they will be rewarded for approved behavior and not rewarded when they do not behave, seldom need any other form of discipline.

DIFFICULTIES OF DEMOCRATIC PARENTING

Since far more parents are attempting to rear their children to some degree by democratic methods, it is necessary to examine the difficulties they run into using this approach.

The major difficulty, of course, is that democratic child rearing takes a great deal of time and energy. When families lived in small communities and worked near or in their homes, parents could attend to their children's needs more immediately. In these earlier days, the authoritarian traditionalist method of child rearing was much more popular, but at least in the United States, a degree of democratic child rearing was attempted and was much more possible when the family lived and worked closely together. In the current urban society, so many parents work outside the home, away from their children for many hours, that democratic child rearing practices do become difficult.

For example, there is what I have termed the "freeway father," who often lives an hour from his work and must commute through heavy traffic, which in itself is wearing and tension-producing. His job may not entail the hard labor his father or grandfather endured, but it produces much more emotional tension. The freeway father may leave home before his children get up for school and return after their suppertime. (One major drawback in living in the United States is these vast distances between our homes, schools, factories, and stores. A rearrangement of our living geography would require a major upheaval, but such an upheaval may be necessary.)

In this drug-using and alcoholic society, the freeway father will very commonly want some kind of relief before he can tolerate his family's demands. On the other hand, the wife and children who have missed him for many hours immediately want his attention and affection. If the wife has been tied down solely to homemaking, wishing her husband could share in the task of child rearing and discipline, it is very likely that she will unwittingly shove many of the problems of the day onto his shoulders before he has even set down his briefcase and taken off his coat. If her patience has run short and her day has ended in open dissension, then the weary freeway father finds himself loaded with conflicts he barely comprehends.

For this reason if no other, the democratic handing out of rewards is not always the easiest and quickest method of discipline even though it may work in the long run. Democratic child rearing takes far more patience than the traditional, authoritative approach.

Often parents have to wait a while for a child to come around and do what they wish. They can instill fear in a child immediately; gaining his or her respect often takes more time. Just as a child has to learn any task through some trial and error, so learning self-control takes time and a certain toleration on the parents' part for temporary failures. Often these failures occur when it is most inconvenient—perhaps parents are in a hurry, tired, have little endurance left, or are out in public where they don't want to spend time disciplining their child. A screaming, rude, and angry child in public is very embarrassing to most parents.

In such instances, parents' feelings may *also* be openly expressed, and need to be recognized by both them and the child. At such instances, say firmly (and perhaps quite loudly), "I am becoming very angry and my patience is getting very short." This warns your child that you may take some angry action at the next occurrence of the displeasing behavior.

Such a statement and recognition of the parents' own feelings is also important because it adds to the recognition of feelings on everyone's part. A parent who is always calm and then tells a child "I understand you are angry," is not to be believed. Certainly *there is no requirement that parents be completely patient.* On the contrary, open expression of appropriate anger at your child's misbehavior is an effective form of parental discipline. Even at this point, however, you need not necessarily become punitive in the traditional fashion. You may follow your statement of anger with the observation that your child is not going to get the reward he would earn for being good. Furthermore, if necessary, parents may use strong statements of disapproval and even isolate children by sending them to their rooms.

Just as social approval, praise, and affection are the ideal rewards, so—conversely—the worst punishment a child can endure is to be socially isolated. This is probably the main basis for imprisoning adult offenders. When a lawbreaker is sent to jail, authorities in effect say, "We can't stand you any longer, and we need to isolate you from the rest of us." In ancient times, banishment was the worst punishment the king could hand out. Temporary isolation is often used in society to allow a person to "cool off." In fact, the term "cooler" is a slang term for jail.

In extreme instances, it is necessary to provide some way for a child to cool off. It is also helpful for parents to have a cooling-off moment. If a child throws a tantrum in the middle of the department store, for example, it is sometimes best for the parent to stop shopping altogether and tend to the child's needs. If the "need" is to cool off, then march the child firmly back to the car or to a private spot where you both can sit silently for a while, out of the public gaze. At home, children may be sent off to their room or otherwise isolated temporarily. "When you've cooled off and can think things through, I will be happy to see you again," says the Democratic Parent. However, such isolation needs to be used judiciously, and only in extreme instances. Sometimes, just a momentary grim silence or turning away is quite sufficient.

The initial and most prominent difficulty with democratic parenting appears to be more open defiance and resistance. Of course, anyone—adult or child—resents rules that limit his pleasures or require efforts that the person believes to be useless. The child who isn't slapped down verbally in anger for defying a parent is not going to obey immediately, but may continue to be sassy and impudent, if not outright defiant. Parents are often disturbed to find their angry child does not limit defiance to "No's" or "Make me" or "I won't," but responds with open vituperation and obscene language, even when they are trying to be gentle and are putting the request in the most favorable and polite form.

The difficulty here usually arises when a parent confuses the democratic approach with pure permissiveness. Actually, a democratic parent does not necessarily have to tolerate insults at all. Should the child come to the stage of openly insulting parents, then something has gone amiss *earlier,* when they should have made a special effort to reward and praise the child for being polite, for being logical, and for thinking things through rather than reacting with emotional outbursts.

A democratic parent may well allow and recognize some expression of resistance and anger on the child's part. This doesn't mean necessarily giving in to such expressions of anger, however. A mother or father may listen sympathetically and agree that the situation "stinks," but firmly make it clear that the child is expected to go through the "bummer," knuckle down, and do the work. Parents should not completely ignore a child's expressions of anger, nor take them as a threat. Rather, they must take every opportunity to praise a child for overcoming anger and going ahead with the task at hand: "I really appreciate that you did that, 'cause I know you really didn't want to," a parent may say, or "It took a lot of courage for you to swallow your pride, back down, and do what I wanted you to do, I really appreciate that," or "I was proud that you held your temper and did the right thing." In these instances, parents recognize the child's right to *feel* anger, without necessarily tolerating open and continued defiance.

When the child continues to be resistant, you say, "I'm sorry you feel that way, and I'll wait a minute until you cool down," or "If you're going to be difficult about it, I guess it won't be done and you can just suffer the consequences." In democratic child rearing, however, the consequences are not usually punishment *per se.* Since the child is being encouraged by rewards, the consequences are that he doesn't receive the reward.

CULTURE SHOCK AND CHILD REARING

Looking back again to the "good old days" when Americans still lived in relatively small social groups, one set of parents did not behave much differently or hold different values than the others. People tended to live together in so-called "ethnic" neighborhoods, with common sets of values and child-rearing techniques. If the family lived in the Protestant Bible Belt, and their children faced them with anything different, parents could blame it on the influence of a different kind of people. But such social isolation does not really exist except in few quarters today.

Therefore, once separation from the family takes place and any child begins to experience a different outside world, a reverse reaction from separation anxiety takes place. Before, the child's emotional development was shaped largely by family interactions. But on entering school, all children encounter different adults and different children, different kinds of behavior, perceptions, and values. They begin to bring what they have taken from these social and emotional interactions they are experiencing back into the family circle. "My teacher says," a child reports, or "Johnny's parents don't make him do that," or "Mary gets to watch TV." Thus, parents are suddenly faced with influences on a child's behavior with which they may not agree, and which they may not even understand.

When children come home and say that other parents have different values and allow their children different kinds of behavior, what they are actually telling you is that the neighbors, too, are Battered Parents. But one set of Battered Parents doesn't know the problems of the others.

The Battered Parent doesn't know that the teacher is victimized, too (and blaming her problems on the "poor discipline at home").

The interaction between the external society and the family is crystallized in homework. The school assignments that children bring home have always been a problem to parents. To the poorly educated immigrant, lessons the children brought home were often a puzzle, even a slight threat. The immigrant parent wished the child to become well versed in the new culture, but the child was likely to reveal the parents' educational handicap. In other homes with educated parents, homework was no really desperate problem. At that time there was no television and very little radio to interfere with the extramural lessons. In smaller communities, moreover, parents were more personally acquainted with teachers and more likely to be free to supervise homework.

Our modern society separates parents from the schools. Moreover, parents may have "homework" of their own, or be preoccupied with other things. Many parents do not seem to realize that there is a dial that turns off the television or the radio. Worst of all, many schools' assignment of homework is not at all consistent. Teachers' schedules change constantly. Sometimes a child is given mammoth projects to accomplish over many months; other times, children have weekly assignments; at still others, they seem to have no outside work at all. Some students seem to get their work done in study hall; for other children it is an endless and never completed chore. Many children ignore assignments and never bring their books home even though the teacher intends them to complete lessons at home.

Perhaps the most difficult aspect of homework involves parents' concepts of the school. Most parents today have only a partial conception of the enormous complexity of the modern classroom. Even young parents seem to have forgotten the kind of school they attended only a few years before. They forget that the lessons during school hours occupy sometimes less than half the per class hour. Teachers spend a great deal of time moving from classroom to classroom, taking attendance, getting the sick child to the nurse, getting notes accounted for on yesterday's attendance, handing out and collecting papers, and attending to a great deal of school business—all of which consumes priceless minutes of school time. Moreover, many people imagine that seven-hour days still exist. Children used to go to school at about eight in the morning and leave at three in the afternoon. In many urban communities, this is no longer so: Poverty-stricken school districts have funds for only four to five hours of classes per day.

The truth is that most American children go to extremely overcrowded classes of thirty to forty pupils, in ancient, overheated, or drafty buildings where they meet with overly educated but poorly trained teachers for fewer and fewer hours each day. As regards education, the American taxpayers are cheapskates. An unusually large share of local property taxes is spent for education in many communities, but these monies are a small fraction of national expenditures. Consequently, the conscientious teacher attempts to cram as much as possible into the child in the few hours available. Many teachers attempt to be policemen, demanding strict order in the classroom and piling on the assignments. Others fall back in despair.

The majority of children rebel against the authoritarian teacher. Even ambitious children become discouraged, ignore the assignments, and publicly declare that the teacher is too strict and overbearing. Actually, many children may admire such a teacher but give up any attempt to keep up with the load of assignments that are handed out. Other children fight back directly or indirectly with mischief or almost bland conspiracy to disrupt the classroom. The consequence is that many teachers pick out those few ambitious and hardworking bright children, ignoring the rest except for the few children who purposely disrupt the classroom.

The experienced teacher knows how to get rid of disrupters: The current popular excuse for continuously excluding these children from the classroom is "psychiatric"; children are labeled "hyperactive" and sent to the school nurse for drugs. The more inept teacher is likely to be inveigled into a battle with those children who are rebelling against the school. By yielding to the challenge of the rebellious child, he or she loses control of the classroom altogether, and is usually faced with a gang of children determined to make life miserable for the teacher and thus avoid the tasks of learning.

Homework is also hell because it is work; it implies that the children have some responsibility for doing something on their own. In this respect, homework fosters the child's independence. By assigning homework, the teacher in essence says, "I've shown you how to do it. Now you go do it on your own." But your child is likely to bring the work home and say to you, in effect, "I can't do this by myself; I need your help."

Again, Battered Parents are likely to yield to the child's demand for help, fearing that they might neglect him and worrying lest he be helpless and fail. Of course, the Battered Parent does not accept the possibility that failure and success are something any child has to learn. Rather, such parents identify with their child and experience his failure as their own. They are drawn into a battle of getting the homework done, in which the child prolongs the homework, complains about it, groans over it, and raises the specter of failure.

In the face of such an attack, it is indeed the brave parent who can remember that the school-age child has the task of controlling the Monster within, resist the child's demands, and say, in effect, "Here's your desk. The lamp is on, the TV's off. Do what you can," and close the door.

Quite possibly, of course, the child who has not listened during the day will not be able to do the work. This student will go to school with incomplete homework and will be scolded for it. Most children do not respond as negatively to failure as their parents might fear: When they realize that parents and teachers expect independent work *and* success, most children knuckle down.

Very few educators expect parents to explain lessons to their children. In fact, most teachers would rather that parents do *not* explain anything to a child, but merely make the conditions of the home amenable to getting the homework done. Otherwise, there is little that any parent needs to do or should do. All children will learn the major lesson that there are things they can do on their own. If children complain that they don't understand the assignment, a parent should then advise them to listen more carefully and read the book again *on their own.* In this way, parents can begin to insist, gently but firmly, that children have responsibilities for learning, that schoolwork is *work* for the child, just as earning a living is work for an adult.

Too often parents sit back, blame the school, and hope that it will do something to make their child succeed. Such projection relieves the parents not only of blaming themselves, but even worse, relieves them of the responsibility for correcting the difficulty. Whatever efforts they might make for attending to the child's studies aren't considered too necessary. For example, they may make perfunctory requests that the children complete their homework—but since children hear the parents blaming the school, they will not comply with their parents' halfhearted efforts. Often these same parents passively permit a child to become a social problem by wringing their hands and blaming society. Of course, this also lets the child off the hook. When the parents blame society for children's misbehavior, the "innocent" children may do little or nothing to control their own shortcomings. Time after time I have heard children complain about teachers who were mean or unfair, who didn't make the lesson clear—and the parents promptly backed up their complaints. In such instances the child feels no need to listen, sit still, or do any homework. Indeed, considering the inadequate schools provided by niggardly taxpayers it is even more important for parents to insist that their children utilize every bit of the teacher's time and energy. The inadequacies of our schools and other institutions, glaring as they may be, cannot be used as excuses for parental inaction. At the same time, parent and citizen groups may have to take counteracting moves in the home and at the local community level. If a child is going to a crowded school that provides only a few hours of tepid education, then parents need to make even greater efforts at home to help educate their children.

For example, one often hears from the child, "We didn't have any homework." Investigation may prove this to be true. Underpaid teachers do not want to correct homework after hours, and so they often do not assign any. (I once discovered that a young mathematics teacher at a local junior high school was giving no homework whatever, but was working as a shoe salesman at a local store after school in order to support his own family.) In such instances, parents should see that the child brings home the book and reviews it even if there is no assignment. Research has demonstrated that children whose parents read aloud to them (even after the child begins to read) learn to read more quickly and accurately. I strongly advocate that there should be no such thing as homework; that all work should be done during extended hours. However, such and ideal is not possible, when there are too many children in the classroom in the first place.

By playing an active role in child rearing, parents project the attitude of "I'm in charge here." A child thus comes to respect parents not merely as authorities, but as effective supporters, guides, caretakers, and leaders. This doesn't change democratic parenting: like any wise administrators, such parents still consult the child and the rest of the family, discover their feelings and motivations, and use these feelings to help the child develop. Being in charge does not mean that parents have to be autocratic or punitive. Rather, the parent who seeks to understand the child's needs and motivations, uses rewards as a method of discipline, and gives support and praise is much more likely to be respected. Parents need not assume a pose of being an undefiable authority, which is only an invitation to rebellion.

HOW TO GET YOUR FOOT UP AFTER PUTTING IT DOWN

Every so often it is necessary for you to withdraw a decision, to change your mind. Sometimes you find that you are dead wrong. Of course making a mistake or wrong decision is not necessarily the worst thing a parent can do, but it is often most embarrassing to deal with. In fact, it is easier for children to admit that they're wrong; a child can fall back on the fact that "After all, I'm only a kid." Adult egos, like mighty oaks, fall with a bigger crash.

Whether or not parents can admit that they may be wrong, can change their minds or compromise, depends upon how much they treasure their pride. If a parent's ego is wrapped up in being a perfect authority who never makes a mistake, then it's very difficult to pick up one's foot after having put it down. The mother or father who argues "I'm your parent, so I must be right," is quite frequently asking for trouble. This type of authoritarian stance is, in the long run, completely untenable. The Democratic Parent instead says, "I've listened carefully to all sides, I've given everything a lot of thought, and I have decided that . . ."

This implies, of course, that parents shouldn't be rushed into making a decision. Children are great at creating crises when everything has to be done "now," and are apt to try to put everything on an emergency basis—mainly because children (and even adolescents) aren't very good at planning ahead. For example, a teenager seldom knows what he or she wants to do on a Friday night until seven o'clock that night. At that time, an adolescent finds out where the party is, who is going to what movie, or merely who's going to the library. Every parent has faced that moment when children bring up something that has to be decided; they're already late for school or en route to some event, or something's overdue. Parents who allow themselves to be stampeded into immediate action or decisions often live to regret it and have a very difficult time later in altering things.

Some of these "emergencies" can be avoided, either by planning in advance or merely not permitting them to *be* emergencies. In any case, parents have to learn that they need not yield. Even though the teenager may scream with irritation and frustration, another fifteen minutes of finding out the facts and even an additional fifteen minutes in having the adolescent run through the conditions under which Friday night's entertainment will be handled won't ruin the evening.

The effective parent *always* says, "Let me think it over," then makes every effort to inquire into available facts. A child must be told, "This time, things are going to be delayed, but next time you will be wiser to advise me of the problem in advance so that we can think things through." Here, the emphasis is on thoughtful consideration of the problem at hand.

Teaching children how to delay, how to think things through, is a major but difficult task. Often it is much easier to say, "Go ask your mother," or give some off-the-cuff decision, hoping not to be bothered further. But here, again, parents need to learn not to be panicked or rushed into a decision that may be worse than merely being late. In the long run, the thoughtful parent who talks things out with an impatient child often has less trouble. What a child is to do, what must happen, what regulations are to be followed, what the time limits are—all need to be thought out and talked over before parents give a child permission to do something. Similarly, if a parent assigns a task, the conditions under which that task must be accomplished, its extent, and the timing all need to be clarified so that there's no misunderstanding.

Some decisions may be made after a few minutes' discussion, while others have to be thought out overnight, so as to give emotions a time to cool and the parents themselves time to search their own souls. Once things are thought through and the facts are in, however, a decision must be made. Thus, if it takes time to make a decision, there also has to be a time at which it must be made.

If parents are to be consistent and responsible people who give their wisest decisions, then changes in those decisions should be limited to three conditions. First, any compromises should be on details, not principles. There may be no fooling that homework has to be done, but a child can work out when and where this task (or any other) can be accomplished. Similarly, when there are good times to be had, there should be no doubt whether the child will be permitted to go: the compromises come on the *conditions* under which the good times will be enjoyed. Even these details depend on parental knowledge of the facts.

Second, parents should make alterations in favor of the child's good times or freedom *if* a child has complied ahead of time and without contesting their requests. For example, a father may say, "You may go play at one o'clock if you've finished cleaning your room." If the child makes no protest, runs upstairs and cleans the room, and comes down having achieved the task excellently by eleven, there's no need to keep her or him in any longer. In fact, the parent should tell the child, "You've done so well I'll change my mind." Habitually changing one's mind as a *reward* is an excellent parental move. This means that there will be fewer and fewer contests over requests and limits, and more and more immediate compliance from a child who feels trusted and approved of.

Third, parents should change their minds when new *facts* appear. If a mother and father aren't altogether aware of the situation, haven't had a chance to see all the various aspects of it, then when new facts come in a change of mind is certainly in order. However, parents must distinguish between facts and "reasons." Children often act as junior lawyers, bringing up additional—but usually specious—arguments. They batter a parent with these arguments and label the parent unreasonable. At this stage, parents *do* need to be firm and review the facts as facts. Again, it may be necessary to say, "We'll make a decision after you cool down."

Children not only deserve discipline: they need it. They are not able all by themselves to develop the self-controls that will be expected of them later as adults. They do need continued hard work and constant attention to their behavior and their feelings. The laissez-faire parent who is merely permissive and who doesn't make a *continued* effort to discipline the child by democratic methods is likely to have a terrible time because, even under the best of circumstances, a child keeps testing parental limits. When parents set down a rule, regulation, or limitation, every child tries to find out if they really mean it. If a parent doesn't reinforce the rules, either with rewards or punishment, then their children aren't going to be obedient at all. Under such conditions, in fact, such children will feel quite neglected; it's as if no one really cared whether or not they behave, and children who feel that no one cares, feel unloved. Thus, children treated mainly with passive permissiveness are likely to continue to be negative, defiant, demanding, and dependent. In truth, *this* is what is meant by a spoiled child: not one who is excessively rewarded or praised, but one who is given no discipline at all.

CHILDREN ARE REALLY FUN

When you consider the struggles parents undergo in assisting the child to develop self-controls and start functioning independently outside the family circle, no wonder many parents ask themselves "Are children really any fun?" Yet the parent who always feels under the gun, who constantly worries, who cannot enjoy children is certainly a loser. *The best way to avoid being a Battered Parent is to actively participate in the very enjoyable task of child rearing.*

The infant depends on his parents for his very existence; the younger child needs them for basic care. In this primarily dependent relationship, there is very little that the adult and the child can do together on an even semi-adult level. There are very few games, for example, that you can play with a three-or four-year-old. Nor is play with a toddler a real parent-child interaction; the parents are amusing the child at his own level.

Nevertheless, most parents find the task of infant care enjoyable. Babies require a lot of parental time and energy, but if not neglected or hovered over by over-anxious parents, babies are a delight—a joy to behold.

Just holding and rocking babies can be relaxing. Observing their development excites parental pride. Both parents find cooing over a baby to be rewarding, for baby soon smiles back and holds out its hands to be cuddled. Fathers are deprived of the sensual stimulation of nursing, but holding baby against a manly chest is a first step toward a strong and rewarding bond between father and child.

After the child enters school, however, there is much

more open exchange. Although the child has previously been a cute object of affection, he or she now becomes a human that a parent can relate to much differently. The latency-age child no longer needs aid in everyday activities. In fact, school-age children resent it if parents try to dress them or give them a bath. These care-taking activities are now *their* responsibility.

Now a parent can do so many more things *with* latency-age children rather than merely *for* them. Conversation no longer has to be limited, as a great deal of the child's vocabulary is already acquired. Children of school age still have many words to learn, but they do so through conversation with adults.

Once the child has learned to read, then even more exchange can take place. Children are now very aware of the outside world and can converse about it with some meaning. Thus, parents will find much more companionship in the school-age child. Moreover, since it is the task of latency to develop self-control, mothers and fathers no longer have to discipline and watch over the child quite so closely.

The very fact that the child at this age is attempting to control the Monster within provides a basis for an enjoyable relationship. Since the child is attempting to suppress sexual impulses in every way, this sexually neutral child is easier to relate to than either an infant or teenager. Parents don't have to worry at all that this child will ask embarrassing questions or masturbate in public (as happens with the 3- and 4-year-olds), nor is the child at all ready for the kind of relationships that develop during adolescence. Children at this age may be a bit emotionally obtuse and naïve—which embarrasses some people a bit at times—but in general, they are quite at ease socially. Very little bothers them, and they seldom really embarrass an adult. Similarly, they are trying to control their angers and aggressive impulses; they are much easier to relate to than an emotionally volatile infant or moody adolescent.

This isn't to say that the Monster doesn't sometimes win. The latency-age child is often physically active, wiggly, and "hyperactive." Nevertheless, children of this age do have much greater control over their activity level and emotions than a preschooler, and are much less rebellious and defiant than an adolescent. Simultaneously, parents do have to encourage latency-age children to *maintain* their own self-controls.

Even though the latency-age child is often into mischief and keeps making demands on mother and father in many little ways, this is a very enjoyable age for both parent and child. Children during this period of growth are able to go out and explore the world with their parents. During these years, it is much easier to go places with children, to explain things to them, and to have them listen. Earlier in life they wouldn't understand, and in adolescence they no longer *bother* to listen. Thus, for many parents, the really enjoyable time is when the child is between the ages of 5 and 12; these years in which parents and children are in a relatively nondependent but not-yet-independent relationship are very few.

In summary, to really enjoy children, parents must be willing to spend time and energy with them. The parent who says to the child, "We had a very good time today. I'm so proud of you," will have a well-controlled, enjoyable child. Mothers and fathers cannot let themselves be thrown by the child's occasional failures in self-control. Rather, parents should offer some comfort in these instances: "Too bad you couldn't control yourself this time. I'm sure you will next time." They have to realize when their children are fatigued and worn-out and be able to comfort them without treating them like babies.

The parent who can become actively engaged in the child's efforts to maintain self-controls often find the task very enjoyable. Again, these activities do require considerable patience, but time after time, this patience is usually rewarded with a spontaneous, happy child. In fact, such a child can lift parental spirits at those times when adult pressures are most intense. You need not be at all victimized by the latency-age child; on the contrary, this may be one of the most enjoyable periods of the parent-child relationship.

8. SURVIVING ADOLESCENCE

With the coming of puberty, the relatively peaceful stage of latency ends and parents face a new and more conflictual development commonly known as adolescence. Although adolescence has only recently been recognized as a stage of human development, some form of it exists in almost all mammalian species. In the great apes there is a brief period after physical maturity, at about age 5 or 6 but before the time of mating, during which the male ape is excluded from the group and lives with other males. The male must fight his way back into the group and contest older males for the young female's sexual favors. The same is true among seals and lions; even in mammals such as bears which do not form

97

social groups or herds, there is usually a period of about a year after the cub matures and leaves the mother before mating occurs. Though sexually mature, both male and female bears spend a summer and a winter of hibernation before mating.

Almost until the twentieth century, human adolescence was rather brief lasting from age 12 to age 15. During the Renaissance, boys about 10 or 11 entered into an apprenticeship lasting for as long as seven years, until age 17 or 18, at which time the boy became an approved artisan and could marry. Girls were kept in the convent or in the privacy of the home for a few years between the actual first years of menstruation and marriage.

The current more extended adolescence—which lasts from approximately age 12 to age 21, or even longer—has developed since the latter half of the nineteenth century. Today's adolescence stretches on into a period that probably should be labeled "young adulthood," often continuing on into ages 22 to 25.

The very fact that both socialization and education have prolonged adolescence means that parental contact has been prolonged too—so that the conflicts that occur in adolescence for child and parent are extended and aggravated. Whereas parents a hundred years ago had to worry about their children only briefly, now parental worries over adolescent rebellion and maturation continue for a full decade. Adolescence seems to stretch out year after year, and parents increasingly wish the child would finally grow up.

This prolonged adolescence in itself constitutes a strain on parents, partly because there is a repetition of the separation anxiety of childhood as the adolescent separates from the family. Nevertheless, from time to time most parents sincerely wish that the children would finally leave and take the conflicts of adolescence with them.

To understand the battering that parents take from adolescents, it helps to realize that this stage of life also has certain developmental "tasks." The chief one is the final achievement of independence from the parents. This push toward independence is taking place in a child who is also maturing sexually and who must achieve apartness from the parent so as to mate and become an adult with his or her own family. Along with sexual maturity, there must be an overall personal maturity commonly called "identity." At times, this drive toward independence explodes into spurts and outbursts of a very forceful rebellion. Adolescents must declare— repeatedly, and in many ways—that they no longer require parental care or guidance.

This process, of course, has been going on almost since infancy. Even the preschool child has said, in effect, "Mother! I can do it myself!"—but this development of independent skills has been piecemeal. Until about age 12 or 13, the child's independence has been largely in terms of skills. The prepubescent child is able to do many things for himself, but isn't really an independent identity separate from the parent. Even the quite self-sufficient 10- to 12-year-old doesn't see himself as separate from the family. Starting with the teenage years, however, the child gradually begins to declare that not only is the parent not needed, but the whole family is no longer necessary. Many cultures have often celebrated such separation by what anthropologists call "rites of passage." Today, the most prominent such statement occurs in the Jewish Bar Mitzvah, in which the boy is declared to be responsible for his own soul. However, this declaration was also made in many other cultures of ancient times. The Iroquois child was isolated in the Long House for at least a year and given training for separation from his parents. The Crow and the Sioux also held celebrations in which the youth had to go into the wilderness, separate from the tribe, and exist for quite a few months without the help of any adult. Margaret Mead's classic *Coming of Age in Samoa* records similar formal ceremonies that separated the adolescent out from the adult.

In Christianity, there are such celebrations as the First Communion. The first date and high school graduation are also somewhat formalized social recognitions of the adolescent's separation from the family. But otherwise, the Western world doesn't give much recognition to the actual stages of growing up. Adolescence has no definite beginning or end. The reason lies in the complexity of modern society. A teenager has to learn such a wide variety of skills both for earning a living and for the socialization needed for adult relationships. Today a person must be much more sophisticated to enter marriage and raise children. Thus, the training for adulthood becomes prolonged, and the need for parental guidance more extensive. In addition to completing a broader and more refined education and vocational training, the adolescent must learn the ins and outs of competitive society. To understand what is required of parents during adolescence, it may help to look in greater detail at the struggles a child is going through.

In effect, the child is giving up childhood. Dropping the nice, comfortable state of being taken care of is quite threatening to most children. Although they may rebel in every direction, they still want to know what's for dinner, whether their pants are back from the cleaners, and whether college tuition will be paid on time.

For example, consider the frantic parents whose fifteen-year-old girl had run away from home. They were pretty sure that she was somewhere in the neighborhood staying with one of her girl friends, but they began to find evidence that she had been in the house in the daytime while they were away at work. She had not slept in her bed, nor was there any sign that she'd taken any food; this evidence was chiefly in the bathroom, where they were sure she'd been using the facilities. When she returned home and her mother asked her, the girl explained that she wasn't really comfortable in any other bathroom than her own: She had postponed all of her toileting needs, including defecation, until the home was empty so that she could use her very own bathroom.

Equally threatening to the child is the gradual assumption of increased responsibility. Although adolescents seek a considerable amount of increased freedom, they often reject the attendant responsibilities. Most irritating and worri-some to parents is that adolescents seem to go off in a feckless fashion, disregarding any responsibility, while seeking only immediate satisfaction. However, the freedoms adolescents seek are not merely for immediate satisfaction: they are also trying to be free to make decisions on their own.

This, too, is quite threatening to both child and parent. Teenagers need to know how to make decisions and need to feel free to make them—yet they often feel helpless in the face of the requirements and knowledge needed to make such decisions. Parents, of course, are used to making such decisions easily and quickly, not only for themselves but for the children. Teenagers, then, have the constant feeling that their parents are still running their lives, but at the same time they hate to accept responsibility for their own decisions.

HOW TO LOSE TO A REBELLION

One of the main assaults parents take is when the older adolescent becomes a rebel against the whole society.

But if an adolescent is to become a successfully inde-pendent adult, it is inevitable that in a sense the parent must lose. Up until adolescence, the child may have defied parental controls at moments, but never basically challenged them. During adolescence, however, the name of the game is to break the bonds with the parents and to challenge parental authority. This process is extremely threatening to most parents—and even to many teenagers!—but is especially dev-astating to the authoritarian parents. If they are determined that their word must be law and cannot be impugned in any way, then the teenager's rebellion will become a bloody struggle in which parental defeat is all the more overwhelm-ing. In those rare instances when the parents are *not* de-feated, they still lose—because a child who fails in his rebellion remains a dependent, powerless adult, still clinging to his parents' skirts or coattails.

For the Democratic Parents, the solution is ready-made if they've been at all successful in helping their child establish self-controls during latency. Passive, laissez-faire parents who fail to insist on any demonstration of self-control get into severe trouble. If they have been overly permissive and given the child no guidance or direction early in life, then the child has no inner resources on which to draw; no self-guidance—in effect, no conscience. Such a child often becomes an adolescent monster governed entirely by impulse and emotion and not accepting external controls of any kind. The teenage years become a terrific battle, and this child usually becomes a delinquent in fact, if not legally. Wondering where they have gone wrong, feeling trapped and helpless, the parents become increasingly guilt-ridden.

Such children—and their parents—need professional help. The bulk of adolescents seen by psychologists today have had little or no parental guidance or control during their latency years. They act like overgrown babies—willful, defiant, yet helpless. They reject any kind of responsibility (especially schoolwork), but make constant demands on adults. Often they force the parent into giving them money and other unearned rewards, always promising to obey, but never remembering any such promises. Such adolescents are not welcomed by their peers, who realize that they are not behaving appropriately and shun them. In turn, these immature adolescents attempt to buy friends—either directly by gifts, or by behaving in an outrageous fashion so as to attract attention. Realizing that their adolescents are not socially acceptable only increases the parental heartache.

Less in danger, but still faced with an uncontrollable rebellion, is the parent who helped the child achieve some self-controls in latency, but abandoned the job when the child entered puberty. A child may be able to gradually separate from the family once latency self-controls are instilled, but parental support and guidance are needed throughout the child's adolescence nevertheless. Especially during these years, it is not yet possible for parents to sit back and beam at their success in child rearing.

Indeed, if anything, the child-rearing job is most onorous during this last phase of childhood. It's not only the stiff-necked authoritarian parent who takes a beating from the adolescent; the Democratic Parent, too, is often on the horns of a dilemma. If the teenager is not set free, then the Democratic Parent too often retreats into an authoritarian corner. On the other hand, should the Democratic Parent continue to allow greater degrees of freedom, there's always the risk that a child will carry the rebellion too far. The adolescent may not be sufficiently sophisticated or controlled to stay within social bounds. Thus, Democratic Parents worry continuously lest their teenager not be capable of the self-guidance so necessary during these years.

This particular aspect of rearing an adolescent demands the greatest care and finesse. In every possible situation, a parent should encourage and support adolescents in making decisions, even though they may prove to be in error or at least embarrassing. Of course a parent must be aware whenever there is some danger to the adolescents' lives or when they might get in serious social trouble that might seriously compromise their further education and welfare.

For example, Karen, age 14, had a crush on her handsome young mathematics teacher. She hung around the classroom constantly and in her notebook wrote secret notes to him that she never gave him—but which her mother discovered. When her mother asked her about these notes, Karen was very put out that her mother had "pried." Yet Karen knew that her mother looked at her homework and she had left her notebook open to these pages on her desk, where her mother passed by frequently. Thus, perhaps Karen hadn't taken too much care to hide this not-too-secret crush from her mother. The math teacher was unaware of how the girl felt, but he too noticed that she was frequently at his desk, offering to do little favors for him whether or not he needed anything done.

Shortly thereafter, Karen came home in tears, for she had discovered that the teacher was getting married. Feeling very rejected, she moped about the house for the whole weekend and could not be comforted. She paid little attention to the girl friends she usually confided in and was utterly disconsolate. By midweek, however, she had resolved to "bravely" endure this tragedy and withdrew all her savings to buy the teacher a wedding present. Her mother advised her that this might not be socially appropriate, but Karen was determined to compensate for her lost love. The mother suggested gently that perhaps her math teacher would be embarrassed by such a present coming out of the clear blue from a little girl. Karen became furious, declaring that she was no "little girl" and that her mother just didn't understand anything. Even though Karen's mother still didn't approve, she decided that it would probably be no great harm for her daughter to go ahead with her plans.

Karen picked out a fairly expensive man's sweater; her mother pointed out that a wedding present should be intended for both husband and wife. Again Karen refused her mother's advice. At the last minute she decided not to deliver the present in the classroom in person for fear that her classmates would laugh at her, and her mother pointed out that Karen's fear of being laughed at suggested that Karen herself knew that this gift was not quite appropriate. Finally, Karen left the gift secretly in the teacher's car.

Several days later, Karen's teacher called at the house to thank her. He acknowledged that he understood how she felt, but returned the present. Again Karen was hurt and wept for several days straight. Wisely, her mother did not repeat what she had already told her; instead, recognizing how hurt her daughter was, she gave Karen a considerable amount of support. She did not flaunt at Karen the fact that she had been right, but sympathized with the child's depression. In a week or so Karen recovered, came to her mother voluntarily and expressed appreciation for the advice she had disregarded and for her mother's love and support when she had felt so badly. Karen assured her mother that she had learned a lesson and was going to "grow up."

This process of becoming a distinct individual may not seem so clear-cut when the teenager imitates other adolescents or participates in teenage fads and fashions. Many parents deplore this imitative behavior and get into conflicts when their teenagers insist on being "like everybody else." But when a teenager joins in teenage activities or fashions, the main idea is to declare independence from the parents' age group, to be young and fashionably separate from the "establishment"—an easy way of rebelling, since teenagers find support from their peers.

Parents who are unhappy with such imitative behavior may wean a teenager away from it by praising and promoting *all* individual rebellion and ignoring the "group" behaviors. Thus if teenagers insist on wearing precisely the same clothes their classmates prefer, let the demand pass—but praise them when they select different clothes or make independent choices. Often teenagers' choice of clothes, manner of speech, and other behaviors may seem quite bizarre, but for them are a quite necessary part of asserting their individuality. As long as this individuality does not harm anyone, a parent should encourage it. Moreover, if a mother or father can let teenagers try out various statements of their own individuality, they'll actually become less rebellious in other ways.

One of the adolescent's most common forms of rebellion is the increasing demand for privacy. In part, teenagers need privacy because of their burgeoning sexual needs. But they also want to assert that their possessions, behaviors, and ideas are an individual matter, separate from the family possessions and family activity. Adolescents do not want other people looking into their rooms, going over their clothes, looking at their notebooks or letters—not that there's really anything to hide from prying and disapproving eyes, but merely because these are the adolescent's *own* things and activities. A comparable situation: Adults might feel insulted if someone opened their mail, even though the contents are something they could easily show to anyone else. For the adolescent, such privacy is doubly essential as an assertion of identity. This privacy includes the freedom to choose—and keep secret—their own friends and acquaintances.

Perhaps no other aspect of adolescent life bothers

parents more frequently than this conflict over their children's choice of friends. Up until World War II, most Americans spent the greater part of their childhood in the same community, where people knew one another's families. In our very mobile and urban society, it's often impossible for that generation—now the parents of today's adolescents—to know the families whose children attend the same high school. A community life based on personal acquaintances is almost unknown in American cities and is fast disappearing in small towns and rural areas. But even in the "good old days" (to which parents too often refer), teenagers didn't want a parent to know with whom they associated or where they were going—merely because the teenagers felt it was their right to choose their own friends and go where they wanted without parental interference. Thus, the questions "Who are you going with?" and "Where are you going?" so often ignite a conflict between adolescent and parent.

It really boils down to whether parents feel they can trust their teenagers. In fact, teenagers often put it on the basis of trust—and quite correctly. This matter of trust is partly resolved if this trusting relationship has been established earlier in childhood. Subconsciously, parents are often asking whether they trust *themselves* to have reared the child satisfactorily prior to the teenage years. If parents feel that they have done a good job all along and have aided children in establishing self-control and an adequate conscience, then it is much easier to take the risk of trusting them to be increasingly separate from the family, with friends their parents barely know and going to places that the adolescents themselves may be unsure about.

For the parent who worries about the company the adolescent keeps or the places adolescents go, there is, of course, no good and reassuring anwer. As a matter of fact, it's probably quite proper for every parent to worry just a little bit. A teenager in a rebellious mood may seek out disreputable people and go to forbidden places. Not that a teenager with good self-control and conscience would necessarily get into trouble with "bad company" or in the wrong places. It is true that even innocent adolescents may be judged by the company they keep, or be arrested for the places they're in. However, the harm that comes to us from being judged or from being legally detained *once* is usually not great. In fact, the practical lesson of being burned by such behavior is often the only way some young people have to learn, since some teenagers refuse to listen to parents.

The question arises whether parents should say anything at all about a teenager's friends or activities. This often starts quite an altercation, in which teenagers stoutly defend their choice of friends. Moreover, it is usually the teenagers' contention that they should be allowed to choose friends without parental intervention. Perhaps in no other area is independent decision more a matter of controversy. Because this choice of friends epitomizes the child's more important long-range development (namely, in decision making), it may be worth examining a little more at length, especially since it illustrates many other types of decision that the child coming of age starts to try to make independently.

Parents often feel that their experience leads them to make a better judgment than their children. Unfortunately, however, the facts are seldom really clarified. The emotions on both sides run much higher and play a much more important place in decision making. As to an adolescent's friends, neither the parent nor the adolescent usually has many facts at all. The parents seldom know much about the other teenagers their children associate with. At best, parents get a glimpse of the friends and judge them on their haircut or clothes, demeanor, or social behavior—if they ever see them at all! Mothers and fathers probably know even less about these teenagers' families or their habits. They may try to find out through their own children, only to discover that the adolescents aren't much better informed; then teenagers become additionally defensive because they don't want to reveal that they know so little about their friends. Thus both parent and adolescent are frequently fighting over something about which neither has facts, only fears and surmises.

Not that some parental fears and suppositions are *entirely* unfounded. When parents see a teenager's friend come and go at all hours without any parental control—perhaps at high speed in what appears to be an unsafe automobile—and when said friend is reputed to have a record with the police, of course alarm is reasonable. Before pushing the panic button, however, reasonable parents try to check out their assumptions, even if this might be quite difficult to do. The difficulty arises in that as parents check out their fears, the adolescents believe that their right to make independent judgments is being violated. The usual retort is "You don't trust me."

Many parents *do* fear that they cannot trust their children. Even though they believe their child knows the difference between right and wrong and will make every effort to stay within the bounds of socially approved behavior, they nevertheless realize that a teenager remains somewhat socially naïve and fear the "children" will be misled. Even if they don't become engaged in some kind of delinquent behavior, a parent will worry that they'll be blamed for the behavior of delinquent friends. Parental reputation, too, may be smirched.

Even more alarming is the fear that the "child" might be injured in some way. Adolescents *do* commit dangerous, thoughtless acts in which others are hurt. All of these things cross a parent's mind—and the adolescent's mind as well!—when the issue of friends arises.

How, then, can parents successfully resolve this dilemma? On the one hand, parents do not want their children to suffer from the acts of their friends, either physically or socially. But they also want their teenagers to become adults who know how to judge others, to know when they can trust people and when to be cautious. How does one teach them to make such difficult social decisions?

Such lessons are seldom learned without some conflict and anguish. It is very necessary for parents to bring up these questions with children long before they become adolescents. Parents must ask a child to think this question through and to raise very difficult questions—to which the parents may not have all the answers. Thus, Democratic Parents must involve the child at a fairly early age, so that by the time the child is a teenager, the question will not become so irritating. If parents *always* make the decision about friends while a young child is growing up, then it *is* likely that the eventual teenager will be quite naïve. Even during the teenage years, however, parents should ask, "Do you know how your friend behaves?" "Have you seen his home life?" "Do you know about his car?" You should explain that you are not making the decision *for* them, but encouraging them to think through the question on their own.

The underlying difficulty is that most adolescents don't always want to stop and think. However, perhaps more important than any other parental duty is that of asking teenagers to stop and consider what they're doing. Of course, this may lead to retorts that your teenager wants to be trusted. But parents can say, in effect, "I just want you to stop and think. If you do, I *do* trust that you'll make a rational decision." If parents have encouraged children to stop and think and allowed them to make some independent decisions before puberty, then there will usually be much fewer conflicts over such decisions.

Nevertheless, it is impossible for parents not to worry some about their adolescents' activities. The teenager is out of sight and out of immediate control, and associating with people the mother and father may not know. No doubt there will come moments when, by parental standards, the adolescent's judgment is poor. Moreover, the best-behaved adolescent can be excited by the delinquency of others and become involved, for the moment, in ill-advised acts. The best parents can hope is that the training they have given their children throughout earlier years will be effective now. For the most part, if parents have provided a solid background in which the child has gradually learned to make social judgments adequately and soundly, then the adolescent will be able to carry on without gross social difficulties.

Nevertheless, even a well-behaved child with good

parents can make a mistake. For example, children may be judged by the company they keep, and their reputations may suffer as a result. A girl who has a sexually promiscuous girl friend may temporarily be judged by that association. Reputations are not permanent, however, and in the long run it may not hurt a daughter to be misjudged. Rather, if adolescents learn that they've acquired an unjustified reputation because of their friends, they will have learned, albeit painfully, how reputations are formed.

Let's take a more serious example: the teenager who is in company with people doing illegal acts such as taking or selling drugs. Suppose that adolescent is arrested and charged with being at a place where such drugs are used. Certainly being arrested is embarrassing and painful to parent and adolescent alike. If this is a single first offense, however, most courts today are likely to either dismiss the charges with a scolding or put the child on probation and remand him back to the parents. Again, the shame and embarrassment may be what some adolescents need to learn their lesson. It may also alert the parents that a teenager needs further guidance in developing decision-making skills.

So far, this problem has been considered largely in terms of threats to the child. Involved in the choice of adolescent friends, however, are other kinds of fears that derive from within the family and the child-parent relationship itself. Parents may really not trust either the child or themselves, being overly anxious that they have not done as good a job of child rearing as they hoped. Now that the child must make decisions outside of the family, the parent begins to worry excessively. Another personal aspect of decision making has to do with separation anxiety. Parents worry most because the child is separating from them; basically they are afraid their child will desert them—the problem is not so much that the child is going to have bad friends, but that he is no longer going to use parents as friends and will be separated out from the family. Many times the chief "bad" aspect of a teenager's friends is that they take him out of the family and into activities where parents and other family members cannot be involved.

For example, one father concerned about his fifteen-year-old son's attending a very popular rock and roll concert could not understand why the boy refused to let him go along. The father went so far as to offer to smoke marijuana with his teenage son, either at home or even in the concert—where it was likely that both would be arrested! And he was extremely upset that his son rejected all these suggestions. At the same time, this father was highly critical of the girls and boys his fifteen-year-old was associating with.

In this case, the boy's father and mother had been divorced for several years, and the son had only recently come to live with his father. The father had not seen this boy on regular visitations, since they lived at opposite ends of the country. Thus, he had great hopes that he and his son would become fast companions—as might have happened had the boy been younger. The real clash occurred over the father's need for a close companionship and his son's need to separate from *both* parents and form independent relationships.

Ultimately, then, a decision like forming friendships does have to be left to the teenager. Mothers and fathers should take the trouble to encourage teenagers to think through the behavior of their proposed friends, and express realistic concerns about the teenager's safety and reputation. Even though most teenagers may reject such parental question raising, in the long run, this does help them start asking such questions on their own. Of equal importance for parents in handling such a conflict is examining their own motivations regarding the control of the teenager. Parents who want to keep the child to their bosom cannot really do so. They must realize that all children eventually have to separate from the family, and much as parents may miss them and feel deserted, it is necessary for adolescents to make this crucial move.

9. SEX AND DRUGS AND PARENTS

Sexuality does not really begin in adolescence, of course, nor does sexual knowledge blossom immediately at puberty. In fact, all children have some kind of erotic sensations since birth. Newborn boys often manifest erections, and little girls may masturbate against their pillows before they learn to walk. However, the infant's early sexual sensations are not at all specific and, compared with an adult's understanding and experience of sexuality, are relatively meaningless. Yet this generalized excitement may play far more of a role in children's emotion and behavior than was at one time thought possible.

Children's knowledge about sexuality gathers piece-meal over the early middle years of childhood. As most books about sex education point out, it's best to answer one little question at a time, as that is all that the child is able to absorb. "Carnal knowledge" is seldom initiated or advanced by any kind of formal sex education. Even when children are told the facts of life quite clearly and explicitly, they do not really understand. Often, in fact, they don't really absorb it or accept the explanation. Their minds are not prepared for anything that their bodies are not ready for.

Not that sex education before puberty is unimportant. On the contrary, sex education is extremely helpful in pushing aside the mysteries and misinformation that contaminated previous generations' sexual attitudes. However, what a child knows and experiences about sex is not so much *fact* as *emotion*. This is not hard to understand: The emotional aspects of sexuality are of far greater importance than any intellectual recognition of certain facts. Thus, sexual know-how is not nearly as important for anyone as the emotions involved in first becoming aroused by the sight of the naked body of the opposite sex, and all the activities which lead up to the sexual act *per se*.

These emotional aspects cannot be taught in a high school class. Rather, they begin to occur in the junior high school hallways, on the way home, in the privacy of boy-to-boy conversations, or little girls' giggles in the bedroom. An excellent example of how children really learn about sexuality is in Judy Blume's little book called *Are you there, God? It's Me, Margaret*. In this book Margaret learns about sexuality partly from her friends, partly from her mother and grandmother, partly just from her own sensations and experiences and daydreams. Thus, parents should recognize from the very start that adolescent sexuality is a highly emotionally charged aspect of life—just as it is for adults.

It is important to remember that the child's model for understanding sexuality is, of course, the parents. Their own sexual actions, reactions, and values set the stage for their child's development throughout childhood and on into adolescence; their feelings about sexuality become the background for the child's future experience. If they are at ease about sexuality, their child will be at ease. If, on the other hand, sex is a threatening mystery to the parents or a fact of life with which they have never felt comfortable, the child's feelings will also be set on edge.

That a child learns about sexuality from the parents is very easy to understand once parents begin to consider it. Yet a great many people have had difficulty accepting the fact that the child associates sexuality *with* the parent. When Freud first introduced this idea, it so horrified the Victorians of his day that they rejected all psychoanalysis. The child was supposed to be naïve and innocent, as if fresh from the Garden of Eden. The scientists who opposed Freud (in some circles this opposition continues) completely ignored the fact that children have natural, physiological sexual sensations, and a great deal of sexual curiosity, and that some sexual play does occur during childhood. They were particularly astounded and shocked by Freud's declaration that children have a sexualized attachment to their parents, ignoring the fact that a mother caresses the child in an almost erotic manner from the moment the child is at the breast. Women now admit that nursing is an erotic experience that stimulates them sexually. When first told the facts of life, nearly all children immediately ask themselves (if not others), "Do my parents do that?" When they understand about pregnancy, they are similarly curious and wonder if they were in their mother's stomach. All these sexual facts become part of the emotional relationship with the parents—which relationship in turn, determines the child's attitudes toward sex.

With puberty, there comes an immense rush of physiological sexuality within the child far greater than in any previous time. This *internal,* physiological experience, along with the facts of life, ushers in the child's sexual maturity. Even before physiological puberty actually occurs, many children have gradually become more and more aware of their approaching sexuality. Thus prior to her first menstruation, a little girl has budding breasts and an increased hip size. Similarly, before a little boy has his first sexual emission, he begins to have some pubic hair, to experience erections, and have generalized sexual dreams. For both genders, talk about sex, interest in sex, and awareness of sex increases monumentally from about age eleven to thirteen. This sexual awareness is aided and abetted by the adults who decided it would be best that pubescent children be separated from the latency children and placed in a junior high school.

Many children in this current "liberated" generation accept pubescence as a pleasurable and exciting experience. Many children look forward to growing up to their burgeoning sexuality. Yet these same children may be considerably anxious about this phase of life and thus approach it with mixed feelings. Even those who outwardly seem to relish their new standing have many moments when they doubt themselves and when the new experience seems frightening. For still others, the whole experience is a crisis they try their best to avoid.

The anxieties accompanying puberty are multiple, but it may help to think of two chief sources. First, the onset of puberty means leaving childhood. The threat here is not directly sexual but rather, again, heightens the separation anxiety present throughout childhood. Children now realize that as they grow up, they'll begin to associate less and less with the family, be more and more independent, and ultimately create a family of their own. They will no longer be irresponsible and dependent children; more and more will gradually be expected of them.

Again, junior high school epitomizes this independence. The child no longer has one teacher to take care of him, but floats from class to class and is assigned work to do independently, almost in adult fashion. She or he is less and less dependent on the teacher as well as on the parent. Children know, too, that they are going to be more and more responsible for their own sexuality. It is up to them to find their own mate, to get out and meet the opposite sex. Sexuality, therefore, is another kind of independent move.

In earlier periods of childhood, there has been a good

deal of open affection between child and parent in which there was unrecognized sexual stimulation. This stimulation is now no longer acceptable, however. Pubescent girls should not sit on Daddy's lap; mothers would not think of bathing pubescent boys, who won't allow Mother even to pat them on the head or give them a goodnight kiss. Kisses and petting begin to mean something that crosses the ancient incest taboo. Whereas previously, affectionate relationships were chiefly between parent and child, they now are directed out toward the world and away from the family.

Thus, sexuality has its threats to the child-parent relationship, and the parent often feels very upset about this. The father realizes that his daughter is no longer Daddy's little girl. He is worried that she is now beginning to attract the glances of younger males. He is even more afraid than the mother that something awful will happen to his daughter. He is more critical of her dress and her appearance. He may also assume a rather joking relationship with his son in which he embarrasses the boy by references to the boy's sexual growth.

Mothers are usually a little more sensitive about these things, though they too may begin to remark openly about the child's sexual development, much to the child's embarrassment. Some parents do not know what to do about their child's new development and joke about it to hide their own anxieties. But if the parent makes remarks about the child's puberty, the child is likely to withdraw from the parent even more. Parents who have depended on affection from their children will find this a very disappointing age. What was once a sweet little girl or darling little boy now becomes a moody, rejecting monster. Not only will the child not permit himself to be touched or caressed; he or she actually avoids social contact with the parents as well.

MY SEX LIFE IS BETTER THAN YOUR SEX LIFE

Another major parent-and-child conflict caused by puberty is sexual competitiveness. Seldom, if ever, do child psychologists recognize the fact that parent and children compete sexually during adolescence, but it is well known in popular literature and myth. The best example is in the legend of Snow White, in which the wicked Queen says, "Mirror, mirror, on the wall, who's the fairest of them all?" realizing that the fairest is her stepdaughter. In fact, it is not uncommon for girls at this age to feel that their mothers are like the traditional stepmother. Though the "stepmother delusion" is more of an attitude than actual fact, the rivalry is quite often there—between mother and daughter or between father and son.

It is a cruel fact of nature that just as adolescents begin to bud into beauty and sexuality, their parents begin to fade. Thus, a woman in her late thirties, facing a pubescent or teenage daughter, may feel her fading looks even more intensely. Similarly the father, getting paunchy, finds his young son with rippling muscles beginning to be fascinated by girls. The father often wonders whether he himself is really still attractive to other women. Such competition between adult and adolescent is seen in apes or seals or lions, where the young male is driven from the pack and is not able to mate until he can fight back and win a female away from the older males. This type of competition is less obvious in human tribes, but among primitive tribes isolation of the young male was fairly common. Even in immediate previous history, young men were sent off to school, to the army, or to sea for a few years until they "settled down," so that they would be less an immediate threat to the male authorities. Girls, too, were sent to convents, were otherwise protected, or were married off at a fairly young age and gotten out of the home.

In short, families in the past usually handled this competition by trying to deny it completely. The parent's usual behavior was to deny sexuality more fiercely than ever before, both for themselves and for the child. This always made it very difficult on the adolescent who felt normal physiological urges and who was under pressure from his adolescent peers to participate in activities which, if not openly sexual, often had sexual connotations. The teenager would find an enormous disparity between a home that tried ruthlessly to suppress sexuality and the surrounding community.

A prime example is the child who belongs to a religious group that advocates suppression of sexuality during adolescence while most of the rest of the community behaves in an almost opposite fashion. Nowadays, adolescents experiment sexually quite openly and promiscuously. The child who doesn't engage in such activity is looked down upon somewhat by the peer leaders. Adolescents are thus under considerable pressure to engage in *some* kind of sexual activity—or at least pretend to. The child who disdains, ignores, or represses sexuality may be in considerable social disrepute. The child who is taught to repress sexuality at home and in church, and then joins with other teenagers socially will be equally in conflict with his family and his church. Luckily, these conflicts are less and less common, but they still occur often enough to give many children considerable difficulty.

Another kind of sexual competition is present in the so-called "liberated" family. Here the adult says—at least intellectually—"Let's accept sexuality quite freely, as a natural part of life." An open acceptance of sexuality does make it easier for the child in many ways, certainly easier than for the child of a family that denies and represses sexuality throughout the teenage years. However, there are again some cautions to be taken by the family who decides to behave more openly and liberally. Few of these families really recognize the amount of discomfort occurring over parent and child's unmentioned rivalry. Thus, parents who parade nude around the house or who discuss their sexual adventures are likely to disturb considerably the teenager who feels that this is inappropriate behavior for a parent. To the adolescent, such behavior may actually seem seductive.

Again, this may be a delusion on the teenager's part: He or she wants to see the mother or father as a parent and not as a sexual being. But quite often, such behavior is the parents' unconscious reassertion of their own sexuality in the face of that of their adolescent. If the parents' behavior is mainly competitive, then the conflict between adolescent and parent will continue.

Again, in the long run the parent is likely to lose. The child's sexuality is fresh and new; the adolescent will attract the opposite sex more easily and naturally. Middle-aged parents are likely to find themselves not as sexually attractive as before and certainly unable to compete with an adolescent. Unfortunately, this kind of competition often breaks up marriages, when either mother or father attempts to prove their sexual attractiveness by extramarital affairs. Divorces are much more common at this time of life, when parents feel their sexuality fading and find themselves with adolescents beginning to be sexually active. And if parents divorce when they have teenage children, it is far more difficult for everyone concerned. Oddly, small children can often accept divorce much more easily than adolescents.

How, then, can parents best handle the conflicts over sexuality at this age? First, by becoming aware of their adolescent's physical growth and of society's pressures regarding sexual behavior. Not that parents necessarily have to agree with all the adolescent world's prevalent norms and values—or with those of the adult world, for that matter. But they should not try to deny that a child may be under considerable pressure to conform to some kind of standards external to those the family holds.

Accepting these facts does not necessarily mean *yielding* to them. Parents should help children accept their sexual growth, both physically and as a natural social development. The social facts may be more difficult to handle, but a *parent needs to assure children that they need not involve themselves in anything they do not want to or don't feel ready for.* Mothers and fathers can help both the teenager and themselves at this point by avoiding any kind of competition. This is a time when adolescents must shine and their parents step in the background. Not that parents must give up their own sexuality, but they should step back and let the teenager have the stage.

Sexuality should be experienced step by step, slowly and easily at an appropriate time rather than on a dare or to conform to peer pressure. Certainly the availability of contraceptives has made sexual adventures less threatening, but not all of society accepts such easy-come, easy-go sexuality. Parents should state their own values as a guide to their adolescents. This lets them know clearly and unequivocally that their mother and father do possess definite sets of values. Yet again, parents must realize that adolescents are beginning to make their own decisions—which may be different from those their elders could wish for. As models, the best mothers and fathers can do is be clear and definite about their own feelings.

ALCOHOL AND DRUG ABUSE

Over the past two decades, adolescents' excessive use of alcohol and other drugs has become a serious problem throughout the world. Of course, alcohol has been used—and abused—in a variety of societies throughout history, although much less among the civilized peoples of Asia and not at all in the Muslim world. Young people's overuse of alcohol has always occurred wherever alcoholic beverages were used. Previous centuries gave it little thought because nearly anyone over the age of fourteen was, in practice, an adult. Up until the 20th century, there was no law against serving alcoholic beverages to adolescents or even children.

When the use of alcohol was prohibited in the United States in the 1920s, the chief violators were adolescents and young adults. The typical individual violator of Prohibition was the college youth with his hip flask. As usual in any rebellion, the revolt against Prohibition was led by the young, who when they became of voting age elected representatives who repealed the Volstead Act. Similarly, it was youth who introduced other drugs into the American scene in the 1960s. Adult authorities ignored the fact that many of these other drugs (marijuana, for example) were widely used in other cultures outside the United States and were relatively harmless when compared with alcohol, which is the most addictive of drugs, whose use results in greatest physical harm. But the production and sale of alcohol is a major industry, of course, and thus any attempts at social regulation of alcohol's use becomes a major political problem.

Perhaps parents are less shocked now than during the 1960s to find that their children indulge in marijuana. Yet the use of this drug is probably no less prevalent than when the American public came to the shocking recognition that their adolescents were engaged in drug abuse. Moreover, there is considerable evidence that alcoholism is increasing rapidly among adolescents, often as a substitute for illegal but supposedly less noxious materials. Some authorities report that children who previously were using marijuana are now more likely to use alcohol rather than other narcotics. Similarly, despite a strong campaign against the use of nicotine, cigarette smoking is reportedly increasing among the younger group. I doubt some of those statistics, however, since common observation shows less public use of cigarettes than ever before, but drug abuse is certainly a problem for both adolescents and their parents.

Alcohol, marijuana, and most other drugs are used chiefly to relieve physical and mental tension, to let the individual relax and enjoy life a bit more. All societies allow some such opiate, and it is a rare individual who doesn't avail himself or herself of such a relaxant from time to time. Admittedly, it's difficult to condemn anything that makes life less arduous and more enjoyable. As many people discovered in the 1960s, some drugs actually expand consciousness, increase sensory awareness, and make life a bit more delightful. Many people are able to utilize these substances in moderation without harmful physical or social effects. Most Americans do not realize that many people in other parts of the world use heroin, opium, and cocaine in mild amounts, and with no harmful results. Very often the people who use these drugs regard the use of alcohol as dangerous! The problem arises when any of these drugs is overused—or in other words, abused.

The noxious physiological effects of the use of alcohol and some other drugs is well documented. Research on drug abuse has never come up with clear-cut answers as to its (probably multiple) causes, but common sense suggests that people who abuse drugs are looking for even more relief from tension and anxiety than ordinary amounts of the drug will provide. The cliché says that alcoholics try to drown their problems, and themselves, in the bottle. I suspect that the abuse even of alcohol (which is quite addictive physiologically) is primarily an attempt to escape accumulated tension, anxiety, and guilt. Alcoholism and drug abuse are not at all "diseases" in the usual sense of the word, even though the medical profession and some other groups who seek to combat them maintain this illusion. Drug abuse is primarily a symptom of depression—particularly among adolescents who can't let themselves admit any kind of depressive feelings. Troubled adolescents will do almost anything to get rid of feelings of depression and anxiety. Quite often, depressed adolescents become *more* active and outgoing, seeking through a good time to avoid and deny whatever anxieties they otherwise might have to face.

The so-called "drug culture" of the 1960s was a welcome escape for American youth who found themselves faced with the horrors of the Vietnam War. For that generation, the future seemed to hold little promise beyond unemployment or death in the jungles. The model for drug usage was set by the general public and by the medical profession in particular, who offered a pill for any illness—and everything was considered "illness." This decade also saw massive use of drugs in the treatment of mental illness. Drugs were the answer, and everyone picked up on them. (It is significant that the street drugs today most prevalent are often pharmaceutical productions, utilized without prescription.) Here again, parents are often victimized by the problems of society at large; their children's behavior is not necessarily related to anything they may have done or failed to do.

In many instances, however, adolescent depression does have its origin in family conflicts. Very often these conflicts go unrecognized and unspoken and thus, in effect, are accepted as almost inevitable by everyone in the family. It's very common to find that no one realizes that anything is wrong with the family relationships until an adolescent is found to be addicted. (Of course, the same is true in adult alcoholism as well.)

For example, Dick G., in his early childhood, was a model child and people who knew the G's admired what seemed to be an ideal family. Dick had two sisters, three and five years younger than he. They were well-behaved children who made above-average grades at school and were well thought of in the neighborhood. Mrs. G. was a devoted member of the church; the children attended Sunday School and the family was thought of as "God-fearing." Mr. G. was seen at church less often, but was known as a hard worker who tried his best to earn his family a good income. The only dissension in the family surrounded Mrs. G's utter disapproval of her husband's use of alcohol, but Mr. G. was never seen inebriated and most of his drinking was with friends in his own home or theirs.

Dick was an active baseball player in Little League and was the prize basketball player in junior high school. Dick's growth was slow, however. Soon most of the other boys surpassed him in height and size, and he could no longer compete in sports so easily. He tried swimming but was not built to be a swimmer either, and by the time he reached high school, Dick was no longer active in athletics. When he had been in Little League, his father made extra efforts to cheer him on, as did his mother and sisters. But at age fifteen, Dick was becoming more isolated from his family. His mother and sisters became more active in the church, and his father had to take an extra job during evenings and weekends and was seldom home.

Dick thus sought the company of his peers much more frequently. His mother was frequently critical of his choice of long-haired friends and ordered them out of the house when they appeared with cigarettes in their mouths. During the summer of his fifteenth year, Dick and his mother quarreled frequently. His father tried to intervene, but was seldom home. Moreover, weary and tense, Mr. G. began to drink even more heavily, and he and Mrs. G. had frequent quarrels over his use of alcohol.

When Dick first started high school, his previously good grades dropped markedly. He began to associate with other students who were also failing in school, and didn't get involved in athletics and other group activities. It was here that he discovered the use of drugs, especially amphetamines. His parents, preoccupied with their own activities and obsessed with their own worries, didn't notice how frequently Dick was under the influence of "speed." He merely seemed more active and louder than before, and slept less, but gave no one any trouble. They scarcely realized how infrequently he was home.

Then Dick was badly injured in an automobile accident while driving a stolen car under the influence of the amphetamines. No one was really angry at him, even after he almost killed himself. Only when he admitted that he had become addicted to speed did the family begin to look at their situation and at Dick's depression. It took several months of family therapy sessions before Dick's father let loose with his anger, cussing out his son for being so irresponsible and for ignoring the values that he and his wife had set up for the boy; he then turned on his wife to display his anger at her for neglecting the boy and being so ignorant of his feelings.

Deeply hurt, Mrs. G. burst into tears, unable to respond to him otherwise. Nevertheless, her tears did represent her feelings very strongly and directly. Strangely enough, Dick was actually relieved: He remarked that he had thought his father was angry at him all along and was happy that he had finally admitted it. It was much easier for Dick to deal with his father's anger than his father's drinking. This enabled Dick to express some of his disappointments in life and his own anger at his parents—feelings they had never realized he had, but which were easier for them to deal with than his use of drugs.

IS THE OUTSIDE WORLD TO BLAME?

Only a generation ago, children could find all kinds of innocent amusement on the streets or byways of small cities. I remember with considerable nostalgia prowling the banks of a small creek in my home town in California, but that creek has long been filled in and paved over. Parents today find themselves responsible for a great deal more of their children's play and entertainment. The days of Tom Sawyer and even Penrod are gone, and the asphalt jungle is before us. Parks and playgrounds are terribly overcrowded and often vandalized, and parent involvement is seriously needed on both the individual and group levels. Only the active, concerned parent can prevent juvenile delinquency.

Undoubtedly, the gross inadequacies in many of our social institutions need correction. Many of these—especially those that bear directly on parents and children—have been discussed throughout this book. Certainly our poorly financed, overadministered public schools need a serious overhauling. The manner in which the legal justice system handles juvenile offenses also needs a complete reworking. The rights of children have never been recognized in court, and courts often assign blame, especially against parents, without any concept of how this might be righted. The institutions for the special care of delinquent and addicted teenagers also run on marginal budgets, and are more often administered by politicians than by trained professionals. There is still almost a complete lack of child-care facilities for working mothers. Many children are ill or in trouble because working mothers have no way of caring for them. Often people able and willing to go to work are forced to go on welfare in order to stay home and care for their children.

All of these social problems certainly affect individual parents and children, but often they seem far beyond the reach of the parent and certainly out of the child's. Juveniles are often the ones who take the lead in rebellions aimed at some of these social ills; yet, for the most part, they leave the individual feeling very helpless. The youth movements of the 1960s didn't in themselves result in social change, but they did arouse many adults to joint action. It may not always be necessary to take to the streets, and certainly violence is not to be condoned in a democratic society. Yet citizen pressure is gradually becoming a major political power in the United States today. If parents blame the schools, then parents are responsible for being active in organizations that will change the schools. If parents feel that drug laws are poorly enforced by the police, then police indifference can be altered only by outraged citizen groups. If there is a need for child-care centers for working mothers, then groups of working parents must unite to let their government representatives know what they need.

Tragedies are often tempered by long-range successes. Children grow up to be happy adults who are successful at what they want, even though it may not be just what you wanted for them. Relieved from the griefs of parenthood, the older adult can go on to live a satisfactory and self-satisfying life, free of the demands that come from child-rearing. Perhaps this is what Browning's poem "Rabbi Ben Ezra" meant by "Grow old along with me, the best is yet to be."

10. SEPARATION WITHOUT ANXIETY

Children need to reject their parents occasionally in order to declare their independence. Such rejections and disappointments add to the very natural separation anxiety that occurs as a child becomes more independent, self-sufficient, and grownup. Many times, the parental hurt feelings are accompanied by considerable depression and fear that the child will separate rapidly and completely. For many parents, the loss of a child's love implies the diminution of their own egos. As the child separates from them, they become depressed and mourn the loss of a little child's undiscriminating and unlimited love.

If parents are not to remain hurt, it is necessary for them to change their expectations. It is not possible for a child to respond fully, every time, to parental affection; the demand for such a response implies a childlike relationship—always obedient, always loving. While children are still babies, parents may reasonably expect them to be utterly dependent and to reward normal attention with unlimited love. As a child grows and develops and separates from the parents, however, then the type of love parents may hope for becomes more discriminatory and, in a sense, limited. The child still loves them deeply, but does not need them every moment. Children may actually love their parents for letting go, for permitting them to grow, for making fewer and fewer demands.

In past centuries, children were expected to follow parental dictates without question. The autocratic family flourished in societies in which everyone had his or her place or class position. Thus, a child was expected to live within a set social circle, and to follow a prescribed religion, trade, and predetermined marriage. Almost from the beginning of the United States, however, Americans declared with pride that each individual chooses his or her religion, vocation, and spouse. By and large, the American educational system gives enough choices such that a child can choose from many different vocations. Americans believe in romantic love and encourage adolescents to make a choice among various possible mates. In the last century, moreover, Americans have liberalized divorce standards considerably so that people may make this choice several times during their life if they become dissatisfied with a hasty or unfortunate marriage.

This tradition was particularly reinforced by the rebel generation that grew up during the 1960s and defied a great many of their parents' values and customs. Perhaps the parents of adolescents reading this book may find their young adult offspring a bit more conservative and conforming, but times change so rapidly that it's almost impossible to predict how one generation will treat its predecessor.

Certainly religion is no longer forced down one's throat, although at one time if a child lived in a strict religious family, he was pretty well expected to follow that religion. By and large, Americans do encourage independent lives and independent decisions, but in so doing, parents' hopes and expectations are often dashed.

Parents may hope that sons or daughters will receive and be able to utilize the finest education, that they will make completely happy marriages, and that they make some kind of decision for spiritual guidance from whatever kind of religion may attract or satisfy them. Yet parents may find that their children turning from adolescence to adulthood make no such decisions at all. In fact, they will likely absorb only as much education as they really want. They may not make any kind of immediate occupational decision, and currently it is quite popular to enter into a relationship with the opposite sex that doesn't at all conform to what has been considered a marriage in the past. In marriage children cross not only the line of religion, but of race as well.

Even the definition of success has changed. At one time, success was measured in terms of money and power. After the generation of the 1960s, however, not everyone considers money the chief criterion of success. For many young people, it's at least equally important to be an emotionally sensitive person who is involved with others, often at the sacrifice of making money or of achieving social status. Such a change of values can be shocking to parents who find it very difficult to accept that their offspring does not even *want* to be rich or powerful.

Most parents realize that their adolescents may revolt against tradition and not accept the kinds of lives that they would have them lead. They assure themselves that as long as their offspring is happy they will swallow their own ambitions and instead try to support the child's independent decisions as he or she grows into an adult. Unfortunately, it is often the hard-working, involved, Democratic Parents who are most disappointed. They want the "very best" for their child and often feel that *they* know what is best. The parent may be publicly proud of a "creative" child, but privately may not appreciate a young adult's decision to be an artist or writer. A parent whose daughter or son becomes a poet or revolutionary may have even greater trouble suffering in silence, even if the poet or revolutionary bothers to earn a living by some routine employment. When the grown children are not a pride and joy—or rather, when parents' pride and joy depend upon their children—it can be very traumatic.

Let's suppose that parents *can* bite their tongues. Let's suppose that parents can assure themselves that their children are planning a life that will satisfy themselves; nevertheless, injury is constantly added to insult. Even though the now-adult offspring choose their own lives, most parents still hope against hope that these young adults will continue to turn to them for advice and support. Young adults may seek parental advice in some instances, or may turn to a parent in times when they are feeling low, but far more often they don't even inform the parent of decisions they're making or of struggles that they're enduring. Often parents feel very hurt that their grown-up children haven't even kept them informed about their lives.

Although elders may consider themselves the font of wisdom, young adults feel the need to have their own experiences in a different kind of world. They regard parents as biased, even uninformed. Not only do they not seek parental advice, they almost seem to skip it. Even when advice is given them, they're sometimes quick to reject it or, at best, politely ignore it. Again, those parents who had given their children the most attention are the most likely to feel bitter and rejected.

The same thing occurs when young adults need sympathy and comfort. To turn to a parent for emotional support would, of course, renew and reinforce the bonds of childhood that have only so recently been dissolved. Thus, it's more common for the disappointed or frustrated young adult to turn to some other person. Again, such a rejection of parental love and support most often occurs when the child-parent relationship was actually closest. It's the strong tie that teenagers and young adults find hardest to break.

If parents have adequately taught their children to be independent, they will be independent emotionally as well and may not turn to their elders later as adults when they are feeling low. It *is* possible that the 18-year-old college student may return home to Mother or Dad when she or he has failed a course or had a disappointing love affair. But if the child is 19 or 20 and has been away from home for a year or more, he or she will likely turn to a roommate or to some other young adult for comfort. Thus, at this point, parents may find that they have been abandoned in a role that they've long treasured. This is extremely difficult to take and often quite painful.

By the time an adolescent becomes a young adult, parents have been involved in child rearing and have had a child depending upon them for almost twenty years. Although many times mothers and fathers may have not too secretly wanted to be free of the burden of the child, there is a feeling of loss. If parents have several children spread over a period of years, the losses will be gradual, but multiple. Resolving this loss and recovering from it depends upon how the parents have been able to fill their own lives.

An overprotective, clinging mother will try desperately to maintain a maternal role, largely because she has no other. In effect, this is the result of the "sexist" social position to which a woman was relegated for thousands of years and from which she is being liberated only now. She was a mother and homemaker only; and when her child-rearing years were over, she found her life dreadfully empty and seemingly useless. Thus, among middle-aged women, depression is a very prevalent disorder that was for too long and too readily attributed to the changes in physiology. The changes in a woman's body in midlife, about the time when her children are leaving, do certainly add to her difficulties. In the sexist tradition, menopause alters a woman's feelings about herself, especially her feelings of being sexually worthwhile. If being a mother has been her whole identity, the loss of her children becomes an even greater factor in her depression.

The years that parents spend rearing children are actually a very short span in their overall lives. If fathers and mothers have involvements of their own—a career, or activities other than child rearing that fill their lives—then the depression that follows when children leave the family will be considerably eased. Fortunately, more women now enjoy a career or other activities outside the home, and are thus less dependent on motherhood for their identity. Even so, the loss of such a core identity remains a severe blow to many a woman, who really has to busy herself to find some new fulfillment.

The effect of this loss on a father is often less visible and dramatic, but often equally intense. The father who has been merely a breadwinner and hasn't played much of a role in rearing his children may not seem to suffer much of a loss. Such a man often feels, however, that he has worked very hard to see that his children "had everything I didn't have" and suddenly he finds that not only have his children gone, but he's never really had a chance to be an active parent who had a direct and open relationship with his children. For such a father, the separation of the child is a double loss. The depression of a man in late middle age often stems from his realization at how much of his relationship with his children has been irretrievably lost.

The luckier father who has had an opportunity to be with his children and play with them, help guide and rear and care for them, also suffers loss. He at least has some memories to assuage his depression and is more likely to have a continued relationship with his adult offspring. The young adult who has never felt much fathering is unlikely to continue *any* kind of relationship with an absentee parent. Conversely, the father who has spent all his time earning a living will more likely judge his children in terms of their earning capacity and be disappointed if they have different priorities than money.

In the long run, the grown offspring gives parents the most respect and affection when they are able to view him or her as an adequate and free adult. It's when parents do not believe that their child is capable that a child rejects the parents, disappoints, or even reviles them. If parents are not to become hurt, their love must be given freely, without strings; without expectations.

If children are to separate from the parents, they need not satisfy parental ambition, build up parental pride, or build up parental ego. Thus, when suffering from separation anxiety, mothers and fathers need to say, "Yes, I'm upset that my children are growing farther and farther away from me, but I'm also proud that they can be independent." Such a parent might add, "Now I need other things to fill my life than my children," and go to seek out other kinds of activities and patterns of life that may not involve child rearing. Parents cannot depend altogether on their children for all their affections, nor will a child necessarily bring them rewards in the sense of achievement. But a child does bring many individual moments of happiness, and it is largely these moments of affection and love that heal over all the wounds that parents endure.

11. THE "SECOND FRONT": GRANDPARENTS

To begin with an example: John and Linda, both 35, lived with their two school-age children in a large midwestern city, where John earned a fairly secure living as a foreman in a manufacturing plant. His work was steady, and his regular hours allowed him to be fairly active in both enjoying and disciplining his children. Their home was pleasant and well kept, but rather small for a family of four.

Linda had had considerable difficulty with both pregnancies and had remained in a weakened condition after the babies were born. Just as she was recovering from a second long bout of influenza, she was involved in an automobile accident that left her crippled for many months. These illnesses were not only a drain on the family's finances, but prevented Linda from being as an effective and adequate mother as she might have liked, and threw a great burden on John to carry out parental roles.

John's father, a retired Navy man, had separated from John's mother just after John and Linda were married. No one knew exactly how he earned a living, but the grandfather seemed to get by on his pension and what he could win gambling at the horse races. Nor did anyone know exactly where he lived, since he moved about from New York to Florida, to California, following the sun and the horses. John and Linda regarded him as a playboy, and were worried at times because he seemed to have a problem with alcohol. He would come into town and insist on treating them to a fine meal at the best restaurant, where he would usually end up quite intoxicated. After no more than twenty-four hours, he would disappear again, and they wouldn't hear from him for over a year.

John's mother had remarried and she and her second husband were in business in a small city in New Jersey. John had always been close to his mother but had seen little of her after he left for college. When he married Linda, his mother came to the wedding, which was when he first met his stepfather-to-be. He continued to write his mother quite faithfully every month, and she seemed interested in his life and in the children. Though they had seen her once on their visit to the East Coast, she had not visited John and Linda for over five years. John's mother usually remembered the children on Christmas and on their birthdays with small and useful presents. Presents from John's father were usually more lavish, but he forgot as often as he remembered.

Linda's parents were another matter altogether. In effect, she had never moved away from them. John had been on his own for over two years when he met Linda—twenty-one and still living at home, both financially and emotionally dependent on her parents. Her mother had been in her late thirties when Linda, the youngest of a large family, was born;

had been in her late 50's when Linda got married; and was thus over 60 at this time. Linda's father was slightly older. Linda's brothers and sisters also lived in the same city and the family were nearly always together on holidays and on birthdays and wedding anniversaries. It seemed to John that attendance at a weekend meal in the grandmother's home was almost mandatory.

Right after their marriage, John and Linda had moved into an apartment in a building owned by her parents, where they also lived. Linda's father was responsible for John's first and only job—in the same plant where the grandfather was a minor executive. Several other members of Linda's family also worked at this plant. John had hoped to go to college after two years, but felt obligated to provide the "proper" support for his new bride. Linda had never worked outside the home and had no skills for earning a living. This negated the possibility that John and Linda might jointly earn a living and that she might help him complete his college work.

Linda's parents continually repeated that a steady income was much better than a college degree. When the first child arrived, the apartment the grandparents had provided proved a bit too small. They offered to force another tenant to move so that John and Linda could have a larger apartment, but John insisted on moving several miles away and purchasing his own home. Linda's parents were critical of his choice of location, since the house was over a half hour's drive away and was too small to offer possibilities of large family gatherings. At the same time, however, one of Linda's older brothers had purchased a spacious home where the family clan could gather, and John and Linda's restrictions were forgotten.

Throughout their marriage, Linda had been in daily contact with her mother, who was particularly concerned about Linda's frequent illnesses. She felt that Linda had always been frail and needed special care. Whenever Linda was ill, the mother would spend most of the day in John and Linda's home and would frequently spend the night on the living room couch if John allowed. John tried his best to separate his wife and mother-in-law, insisting that the mother did not need to visit so frequently and was, in effect, spoiling Linda. Linda agreed with him but could not, by herself, convince her mother to stay away.

Most of John and Linda's marital dissension arose over the role that the grandmother tried to play in the family. Occasionally John quarreled openly with his mother-in-law and she would leave, haughty but hurt. Linda's brothers and sisters, who suffered similarly if less frequently from their mother's incursions, also tried to convince her to be less protective and invasive in Linda's life. After Linda's accident, however, there was a practical need for further help and John let his mother-in-law stay in the home steadily for almost a year. Linda's father had recently died, and thus the mother had no other obligations. Both Linda and her mother were quite depressed by the father's death and it was likely that Linda's depression prolonged her recovery period.

It was difficult to criticize Linda's mother, a very cheerful and vigorous old woman who seemed to enjoy waiting on the entire family hand and foot. She was up before the others and had breakfast on the table, making sure the children were dressed and out the door for school almost before John realized what was going on. She waited on John similarly, saw that his coffee and eggs were just as he liked, and his newspaper at hand.

One would have thought that Linda would have blossomed under her mother's care, but strangely enough, Linda seemed to become more weak and sickly whenever her mother was in the home. Linda's mother never intervened at all in the discipline of her grandchildren; on the contrary, she provided many small treats, extra snacks, special presents, and even did some shopping and paid for their clothing out of her purse. John also suspected that she bought some of the groceries, especially any extra food treats. However his mother-in-law was fairly well-off in her own right and of course had no expenses while living in John's house.

Since life was so very comfortable, it was hard at first for Linda and John to realize how much the grandmother was dominating their lives. Although never an open disciplinarian, she nevertheless had a subtle influence on their children: She clucked over their misdemeanors, and they seldom, if ever, crossed her. Only when John and Linda decided to take a long-delayed summer vacation with their children, leaving the grandmother at home, did they realize what a central figure she had become in their family. Quite hurt that they had left her behind, Linda's mother even offered not only to pay her own way but to finance the whole holiday.

John often wished that he could be more independent of his mother-in-law, but felt that if he protested, it would seem that he didn't appreciate all she was doing for them. During their vacation, he discovered that Linda felt very similarly. On their return, they were able with the help of some of Linda's brothers and sisters to convince the grandmother to move and find a life of her own. Even though she tried not to show her feelings, they knew she was hurt and angry. The children were quite sad to see their grandmother leave and didn't at all understand why their parents had taken this stand. For a month afterward they continued to wish that grandmother was still there, and visited her frequently.

The children's continued attention and the fact that Linda's family still frequently gathered together seemed to assuage the mother's hurt feelings, and within a year Linda's relationship with her had returned to normal. Linda no longer called her every day, however, and she and John were more likely to excuse themselves from family gatherings when they didn't feel like going.

There are no good statistics to reveal grandparents' involvement in family life, but my guess is that over a third of families have little or no contact with either pair of grandparents. In our current, very mobile society, parents quite commonly move away from their own homes, and their contact with their parents is erratic.

In more stable sections of the population, grandparents may live in the same community and be seen more frequently, but still don't actually get involved in the rearing of their grandchildren. Contacts between the generations are more likely to occur during holiday celebrations or at times of illness or emergency, when the grandparents may help out.

The third and probably the smallest group are those families in which grandparents are a part of daily life. (This group includes grandparents who live by themselves but who are contacted once a week or more and who are in the parents' homes almost as frequently.) This type of grandparent is really a member of the family and influences the child rearing. At one time the grandparent role was such an integral part of family life that a book on the Battered Parent would have made this subject a primary target. Today, however, grandparents usually play a minor role in child rearing. The once very common phenomenon of the live-in grandparent is now exceedingly rare, especially in urban life. However, I would estimate that among Battered Parents, grandparents frequently do play an important role. When parents are feeling harassed, it is likely that they will turn to their own parents for some kind of help. The reverse is also common—when grandparents play a dominant role in family life, parents are likely to be victimized.

The example of John and Linda graphically illustrates two general problems that arise wherever grandparents play a prominent role in family life. The first of these is called "Let Grandma Spoil You" and the second is "Don't Dump on the Grandparents."

"LET GRANDMA SPOIL YOU"

In American family life, it is almost traditional for grandparents to "spoil" their grandchildren. In the first place, grandparents are usually unwilling disciplinarians and are not likely to make demands on the child for any kind of conforming behavior. Even when grandparents may have tended to be autocratic and harsh with their own children, they find all sorts of excuses to relax and retire from being disciplinarians. They're more likely to put up with momentary naughtiness, and if the children get out of hand, the grandparent may return them to their parents for care and discipline. Second, grandparents seem to indulge in extra treats and special care. Grandmother's cookie jar, extra-special foods and special entertainment, extra gifts, and toys are frequently provided.

Such behavior causes no real problem if it happens infrequently, such as on holidays or on visits; but it becomes a problem when grandparents are more a part of the family life. If they baby-sit once a week, if parents and grandparents are in contact several times a week, this spoiling is more likely to take place but even so, likely to be relatively innocuous. The chief problem is that if the children can do as they please at the grandparent's with little or no disapproval, they're less likely to conform to parental discipline at home. Sometimes the spoiling grandparent actually deters child training.

"DON'T DUMP ON THE GRANDPARENTS"

Spoiling grandparents commit their crime voluntarily because of a need to be loved by their grandchild and also so that their own children will see them in a more kindly light. Often, however, parents' behavior at least condones if not encourages that of the grandparents. Especially if both parents have to work, it is very natural to call upon the grandparents to help out. Most often the grandparents do make themselves available, even when weary or ill.

As grandparents grow older, they have less energy available to care for active children—and they may inadvertently spoil a child merely because they do not have the energy or motivation for discipline. They are more likely to let children run wild merely because they don't want to chase after them. It is difficult for grandparents to spoil grandchildren *consistently*. At times, they may despair because their grandchildren don't obey them. If they reared their own children in largely authoritarian style, they may be unable to shift if their grandchildren have been raised in more democratic fashion. Moreover, authoritarian child-rearing requires far more energy than democratic child-rearing. The grandparents then are likely to sink into a laissez-faire relationship with their grandchildren, while deploring how bad they are.

When grandparents are ill or elderly or weary, children's activities necessarily must be limited. Especially if the grandparents are beginning to lose their hearing, children's high-pitched voices often make their ears ring. There are even differences between the body temperature of a child and that of a much older person: the child's is a bit higher than that of his grandparent who needs a warmer room without drafts. Grandfather needs his sweater on, and his grandson needs fresh air and room to run.

For all these reasons and more, grandparent care of children should be kept to a minimum. It should be an enjoyable task, rather than an odious one. If parents continually dump their child on the grandparents, he or she begins to feel like a burden to both his parents *and* grandparents. The child is likely to feel deserted by the parents and thus arrive at the grandparent's home cross and upset. The child's behavior is then likely to invite more spoiling from the grandparent—or more rejection. Often the child subconsciously realizes that the grandparent's extra presents are compensations for the fact that the parents must be away working or on other errands. Again, the child is likely to contrast the grandparent's permissive attitude with whatever discipline his parents try to enforce at home.

THE TIES THAT BIND

Since this is a book for parents, I haven't brought up the issue of grandparents who need caring for themselves. As grandparents age, they may be an additional burden on parents and thus interfere with family life in general. If there are ill and aging grandparents in the home who have to be cared for, then parents attention may be turned away from the children.

Sometimes a grandparent becomes an extra child in the home to be cared for—in effect becoming a rival for the parent's time and energy. This situation is much less common than it used to be, but it still may be a rather severe problem that limits the freedom of the whole family. In such instances, parents should seek outside care. In recent years at least, our society is beginning to provide various kinds of care for the elderly so that they need not be burdens on their adult offspring. Of course, many people feel that the care of their elderly parents is their personal responsibility and are reluctant to seek help from other agencies. However, where a choice has to be made between young children in the family and the elderly person, help from outside is usually necessary.

None of this discussion is meant to imply that grandparents should not or cannot actively participate in child rearing. In many instances this participation is largely positive; the grandparents may assist in caretaking and even in guidance and discipline *if* the relationships between parents and grandparent are settled and the nature of child rearing is clearly defined and understood by everyone concerned.

For example, spoiling the grandchildren can be acceptable if it isn't excessive and, more importantly, if everyone recognizes that this is what is going on. Thus, grandparents who enjoy treating their grandchildren to special entertainments should discuss this with the parents and have a clear understanding when they may be possible and when it's out of line. Before planning such special events or giving extra presents, they should ask the parents' advice and permission. Similarly, parents should advise grandparents when certain discipline or training is necessary and ask their cooperation in carrying out such discipline and training when children are under their grandparents' care. Most grandparents would be willing to assist in this job if the task is clearly defined by the parents.

Conversely, the parents must support whatever rules
and regulations the grandparents wish to impose in their home
while the children are under their care. Grandchildren need to
see their grandparents as adult authorities, and not merely as
servants who rush to the refrigerator for food every time they
are commanded to do so. Most of all, there must be an open
agreement between grandparents and parents as to the amount
and kind of care they want to provide. Grandparents can
continue to aid in the children's care when the parents are
otherwise burdened, but dumping kids on the grandparents
must be limited, just as *they* must be limited in whatever
invasions they try to make into family life without being
asked. If such agreements and understandings are made clear
within the family, then children can be a joy to the grandparents and help fill out their lives.

12. THE BATTERED MARRIAGE

FOR THE SAKE OF THE CHILDREN

Most of the above considerations about child rearing assume an intact marriage in which parental dissension is minimal. But many observers agree that the idealized and romanticized nuclear family of the 19th and early 20th centuries seems to be gradually disappearing. In our urban communities, where there is a high rate of mobility, it's extremely difficult to maintain the same kind of family life idealized at the turn of the century. The time is fast fading when the breadwinner father was quick to say "Ask your mother!" Child rearing and home care are now being disowned by many women, who see other kinds of careers for themselves. A united family that spends time together becomes increasingly difficult to maintain. There are fewer and fewer things that family members can share. Every marriage has strains and conflicts that vary considerably in degree and intensity. Yet today's marriages do seem to have increasing amounts of both. Adjustments to a new kind of shared marriage are not being made quickly, and many fathers are unable to share parental roles equally with their wives. During this time of flux and change, marriages become most unstable. Stresses become intense and widespread, and many marriages dissolve.

Even though the nature of family life and marriage is changing, people still cling to the ideals of previous generations. Most couples are determined to make it "stick." Even when they are no longer in love and relate almost perfunctorily, in most instances a husband and wife will try to maintain an intact family life "for the sake of the children." Although in too many instances, this becomes a hollow phrase, there's something to be said for a family that at least attempts to have an intact couple available to the children. Family life, especially the child care and child guidance, needs to be shared by both parents.

Not that all marriages should be preserved where children are involved, but the breakup of a parental union should not be made hastily or lightly. The value of a pair of parents, no matter how inadequate they may be at times, is not to be dismissed. In many instances, having two parents who may not be very mature or effective is usually better for a child than having only one—or none.

When the central emotional relationship between the couple has vanished, though, it is usually quite difficult to hide it from the children. The parents may be very careful not to quarrel openly, yet even very small children are usually aware that Mommy doesn't love Daddy anymore. Children recognize that whatever open affection was demonstrated is now perfunctory at best and probably has disappeared altogether. Parents may maintain a silent, edgy hostility. In such instances, children may try to bring them together in some way. They may do this openly, by clinging to both parents at once and by making all sorts of overt moves to have the parents begin to show some affection again. Such performance is very common among little children, who will try to snuggle with Daddy and Mommy together.

When a marriage no longer exists in fact, although it may be legally maintained, it is very difficult to carry out parental activities. If husband and wife don't enjoy being with each other, it's difficult for them to enjoy their children together. Very likely, if they disagree over many other things such as money or sex, they are also disagreeing over child-rearing methods. Children begin to experience this dissension when Mother demands one thing and Father disagrees and tells them something else, or when one parent will decide that the other should have certain duties and thus refuse to do anything about the child's needs because the other parent should assume the responsibility. If a mother decides that she's had enough of carrying the whole job by herself, she may actually abandon the children temporarily, hoping that her husband will realize that his children have needs he should be answering. If the father is too busy with his job or other activities to engage in child rearing, then the mother may see him as an "S.O.B." and begin to make open complaints to the children about his neglect.

The situation is most difficult when the parents' dissension does center about the child and his upbringing. The greatest tragedy occurs when one or both parents didn't really want the child in the first place—an occurrence that is much more frequent than many people admit. At times, people have children for very selfish reasons: in order to bind a marriage together, for example. A woman who fears that her husband may desert her may let herself become pregnant under the delusion that she can thereby repossess him. She really doesn't want a child otherwise, and her husband will unconsciously realize that he is being trapped. This child is almost doomed from the start. The parents hate themselves for having the child, and hate the child for its very existence. Often such children are severely emotionally disturbed, or become emotionally disturbing to others.

Frequently, when an uncomfortable marriage is becoming increasingly strained, one parent will turn to a child for support and comfort. When a woman feels that her husband is gradually drawing away from her, she may seek the affection of one of her children as a substitute for the vanishing mate. Of course, the same can be true for a father who finds that his wife doesn't love him anymore and who then turns to his daughter or son for affection. Similarly, a disaffected father may select another child on which to vent his anger against the spouse. One parent's "favorite" child may become the other's scapegoat. Sibling rivalry becomes heightened as children are pitted against one another, albeit quite unconsciously. A child may accept this position of "favorite" of one parent in some instances, but the relationship is so impossible that in the long run the child suffers considerably and reacts to defend himself.

Thus, a marriage that isn't working for the couple doesn't usually work for the children either. In most instances, many of the activities necessary for child care, child guidance, and child enjoyment are aborted or entirely absent. Of course, such a situation is felt by the child, who usually fights back in some way or another. The mother who looks on her little boy as a substitute husband may find that he responds valiantly to defend his mother, but he must break with her when he reaches adolescence or the two of them will drown in the relationship. The mother thus suffers even greater pain when her son separates during later adolescence. Should the son *not* separate from his mother, he may forswear all other relationships with women and devote the rest of his life to her care. Such men often feel trapped by their mothers and project their anger onto other women—often one of the reasons why men become homosexual. They may also seek relationships with other men because they feel deserted by their fathers, against whom they may also bear a grudge.

A similar pattern occurs when a father-daughter relationship is made to compensate for a broken marriage. These facts of life are better described in drama and literature than in psychology books. A prime example is illustrated in Arthur Miller's play *A View from the Bridge,* in which a man tries to compensate for his inadequate marriage and sex life by devotedly "defending" his daughter against all of her boyfriends. In a dissolving marriage, such a relationship is not restricted to parents and children of the opposite sex. Mothers may cling to their daughters in a grand alliance against the deserting husband-father. Certainly, a father can decide that all women are fickle and that he alone is the proper parent to raise his son. Not that the father should not be the custodial parent at times, but there should be an examination of the relationships that develop between parents and children when marriages are severely strained.

THE CHILD FIGHTS BACK

Since a shaky marriage severely threatens the offspring, most children will make many efforts to divert the threat or otherwise try to heal the marriage. Really small children often approach parents and openly ask them to love one another once more. However, the child's more usual defense against the home's dissolution is to create some kind of diversionary problem to attract the parents' attention and bring them back into family life. If the parents are separating, the child may do all sorts of things in order to prevent it. School failure, hyperactivity, delinquency, narcotics, and even suicide are some of the major tactics children use when their parents' marriage seems to be falling apart.

A very common reaction (especially among younger children) is for the child to become physically ill, showing a depression in somatic symptoms. The infant may become "colicky." Strictly speaking, there is really no disorder called colic, only a set of behaviors by which the child reveals acute anxiety and upset. The infant who finds that mother is tense and depressed over her marriage, or that father is absent, distant, or short, will often react by being whiny, by sniffles, and by sleeplessness. The child may be a poor feeder and not develop properly at all. As anxiety in the family increases, so will the child's symptoms, perhaps making both parents unite in their common concern over the child's health. In child guidance clinics, when a couple brings in an unhappy and depressed child it is almost the rule that the counselors should take a close look at the marriage.

Another common reaction of children is to slow their development and start failing in school. Textbooks about reading seldom give more than a mention of the depressed child who stays home or avoids schoolwork because he's afraid that his parents are going to divorce. Yet one of the most common reasons why Johnny can't read is because his eyes are full of tears. Children who are unhappy at home, who feel that their parents are about to separate, can no longer maintain interest in their schoolwork. They leave in the morning feeling depressed and unhappy. They quarrel with other children, pay little attention to their lessons and, with a heavy heart, come home, where they spend hours hoping to find a greater degree of happiness in some way, but *not* in doing their homework. A dissolving marriage is often first revealed when the children are so unhappy that they start failing at school.

Other children may fail at different tasks. Sometimes the anxiety is shown directly, in an increased activity level. One looks in vain for the imagined "brain damage" of the hyperactive child, but if the same doctors would look at the stress and strain of the family life and the marriage, they would often discover why children have a high activity level. A child worried about his parents' marriage doesn't sleep well, doesn't sit still very easily, and is often on the run.

Another common reaction—and diversionary tactic—of the child of a battered marriage is to become delinquent. Many times, children have frankly confessed to me that they got into trouble because they knew that their parents would be concerned, believing that their parents would stop fighting and begin to pay attention to their needs instead. Thus, a child unhappy at home may run away in the hope that his parents will let their marital dissensions lapse, search him out, and comfort him again—a very common daydream among runaways. Similarly, the child who gets into other social problems seeks to disturb his parents in such a way as to make them become family attendants again.

Even a child's use of narcotics may signal that the parents' marriage is failing. The adolescents who turn to drugs for solace or thrills may be trying to get a mother or father back again by getting themselves arrested. Most serious, of course, is the child who finds no other forum for displaying his unhappiness and makes a suicide attempt; but many other behavior symptoms of childhood reflect a conflict in the parents' marriage. Again, where this conflict centers directly around the child and his own behavior, especially over the child's very existence, emotional disturbance may be most severe.

"LET'S YOU AND HIM FIGHT"

Although nearly every child will try to avoid the conflicts in his parents' marriage—at least to stay out of the way, if not make some kind of diversionary tactic to prevent quarreling— the same child may at other times take advantage of the lack of parental agreement. Even in the best of marriages, nearly every child will at times make efforts to divide and conquer. He or she plays one parent against the other, sometimes— especially among younger children—in a very direct and simple fashion. The child who asks one parent for something and gets turned down may then go to the other parent, who hasn't heard the request, hoping that the second parent will say yes. These tactics are so common that most parents recognize them right off and check with each other before some untoward decision is made. When a marriage is headed onto the rocks, however, parents normally don't communicate too well. Thus, it's more and more possible for a child to ask something of one parent and then "appeal" to the other. If a wife thinks her husband is unduly arbitrary with the children or with her, she may passively permit her children to do things that their father has forbidden. Conversely, he may attempt to buy off his children with presents, gifts, or permissions that Mother thinks is not best.

The roles may be reversed in any direction, at any moment. Very often when there's a good deal of marital dissension, both parents may be equally arbitrary one moment and then overly permissive the next, in successive waves. Often when both parents are inconsistent, their child rearing becomes based on their own moods, depressions, and hurts.

For example, a mother who feels very hurt by her husband may look up to see his "spitting image" in front of her and lash out with bitterness and hostility far beyond any discipline her son may require. Fathers may act with unnecessary harshness toward their children because they want to get even with their wives.

Children react to these situations with anger of their own. If not openly enraged, they become more easily upset and demanding, more whimpering and naughty, more defiant and more ill. Where there's more than one child in the family, the sibling rivalry increases to the point of continuous war between the children. Not only do these reactions draw some parental attention (albeit negative), but it relieves some of the anger that the child cannot express directly to the parent. Moreover, when there is such a high level of parental dissension, there's usually little affection available to the children, who fight over every scrap of parental attention. When children are brought into child guidance clinics because of intense sibling rivalry, there's usually an equally intense (if not too overt) marital dissension.

The marital discord becomes a family scrap in which hostility spreads in every direction; everyone feels hurt, everyone is victimized, and everyone loses. When all hell breaks loose, the underlying marital dissension will soon be out in the open and if the parents haven't already sought out some kind of psychological help, the children will usually force them into seeking such therapy.

"WHAT DIVORCE?"

The American ideal is a happy marriage with a happy family. Dissension is anathema to this romantic picture, and thus most Americans would like to escape the conflicts that arise in any marriage. Therefore, the usual approach to marital conflict is a three-step denial. First, the couple tends to deny that there really is any problem. Second, when they can no longer deny the conflict and dissension, their answer is to deny that they're of any importance. At this point, each member of the couple is likely to say, "Oh, everybody fights in every marriage, and our little quarrels don't really count." Finally, when the couple makes no effort to acknowledge or resolve their conflicts, there is the third stage of denial: "Well, nothing can be done about it, anyway."

Thus, in Divorce American Style, a couple actually on the verge of separation may appear to the outsider to have a perfect marriage in which there are no quarrels. Their friends know only that the couple has been drinking too heavily and haven't always been seen together in public. Quite often these couples won't even advise their own parents that their marriage is going on the rocks. However, if there are children involved, usually the children unconsciously know that something's wrong in the family. Children's behavior is the main evidence of unhappiness, and many of the symptoms discussed above will have already begun to appear. Because the children are very often the ones who have openly expressed the unhappiness through their behavior, they feel to blame for the marital dissension itself. Thus, if a boy is being extra naughty, is failing in school, or even feels ill, he sees his parents quarreling over his *symptom* rather than over the basic difficulties in their marriage, and begins to feel very guilty when the marital dissension becomes overt: such children may almost consciously believe that it is their fault that their parents are quarreling.

It is equally common for children to join in their parents' denial of the marital breakdown. Even though they may show every sign of being very unhappy, both in their behavior and in their dreams, they will deny outright that they are aware of any parental dissension. In interviewing children while a divorce is occurring, it is indeed remarkable to find the children expressing such great surprise that their parents are separating. They insist that they've never heard their parents quarrel or ever had any idea that something was wrong with their marriage. Yet they know, at least preconsciously, that all is not well.

The same child may be black and blue from beatings; may be quite aware that the parents have actually fired guns at each other; may know that one parent has disappeared from the home for a long period—yet this same child will say that he or she has no idea that a divorce was going to occur! It's as if children could make themselves deaf, dumb, and blind to all going around them in order to avoid the intense anxiety they would otherwise experience at the thought that their home was breaking up.

HOW TO PREPARE CHILDREN FOR DIVORCE

When such disturbances take place within the family, parents need to take several steps. First and foremost, be honest and admit that something *is* going wrong. Parents need not blame themselves in any way, but simply acknowledge that the marriage is in danger and that their children are suffering. *Acknowledging the problem is the first major step in its solution.*

Second, parents must find some kind of counseling for themselves *and* for their children. Third, in acknowledging the problem and seeking help, they need to have an open discussion with their children of the facts of the marital dissension. These steps will often relieve the children, who then don't have to join in the denial game, having perhaps already realized also that their parents are upset and depressed.

Children will be reassured considerably if parents say, in effect, "We're doing something about it. You aren't to

blame, and you don't have to do anything about it yourself."
A child who realizes that the parents are making some attempt
to solve family problems won't have to take diversionary
tactics or become ill. Not that the marriage will necessarily
continue, or that divorce is bound to occur; the child knows
only that action is being taken about the problem. Children
should be kept openly advised of what is going on so that they
don't live with unspoken mysteries, fantasies, and guilt.

A child does not need to know *every* detail of the
parental dissension, however. Usually it is enough to advise
the child openly and directly that Mommy and Daddy are not
getting along well—that, indeed, they are unhappy about it,
and recognize that the child may be unhappy, but that they
are going to try to do something about it; to resolve it if at all
possible. (Of course, parents shouldn't share with children all
the secrets of their sex life.)

If the marriage is likely to be dissolved, then parents
should advise their children that a separation is in the offing,
try to comfort them, and reassure them that even though the
marriage may be dissolved, their needs will still be answered.
At this stage, each parent should listen carefully to the chil-
drens' questions and complaints. Very likely children will
continue to try to deny that a divorce is necessary, but may be
reassured that *they* do not have to make this decision. Rather it
will be something that the parents and court will make,
independently of them.

There may be many little questions a child may have,
such as what will happen to the family dog, where his or her
possessions will be, who will live in which house, and so on. If
parents do not immediately know the answer to these questions, they must at least tell the child that these questions will
be considered.

Preparing children for a divorce is quite necessary to
spare them further disturbance and pain. For further advice
about preparing children for a divorce and for helping them to
adjust afterward, the child should read Dr. Richard Gardner's

The Boys' and Girls' Book About Divorce, and for parents, *The Parents' Book About Divorce*. For younger children, *Divorce is a Grown-Up Problem* is most helpful. Children who are prepared for the divorce may show considerable amount of anxiety at first, but in the long run, those children will find it much easier if the parents keep them informed of their actions and help them understand clearly that essential needs will be met.

13. THE DIVORCED FAMILY

The pattern of denying family dissension will most likely begin to be relieved once people begin to recognize the fact of divorce and the existence of divorced families in American life. Statistics vary considerably, but it is agreed generally that in the United States in the latter half of the 20th century, about every other marriage is ending in divorce. Not all these couples have children, but one estimate given in Los Angeles County (where the divorce rate is even higher) is that approximately 600,000 children—or about 20 percent of the children in this area—are involved in custody decisions in the Domestic Relations Courts. Without doubt the "nuclear" family of two generations ago is no longer the only type of family to be considered. If these Los Angeles County statistics are representative, then approximately one child out of five lives in a divorced family.

These families vary extremely in composition. There are single-parent families in which the father (sometimes the mother) has completely disappeared from the scene. In other cases, the two parents live separately, neither of them remarrying. More often, one or the other or both will have remarried, and the child then has stepparents as well as parents. (The stepparent's role is discussed in greater detail in Chapter 14.) Sadly, child guidance clinics traditionally prefer to see children of "intact" families. For the divorced family, there has been little or no counseling available.

When parents dissolve a marriage, they do not dissolve their relationships with their child. After a divorce, each ex-spouse remains a parent, and each parent still has obligations toward the child. Very often, divorced parents have to make mutual decisions regarding their child's welfare. Thus, even though both parents feel somewhat relieved at being separated and no longer involved in direct interaction with a spouse they cannot endure, they find themselves brought back together again, willy-nilly, by the child.

In itself, of course, the legal fact of a divorce does not at all relieve the anger, bitterness, and hostility a divorced couple commonly feel toward each other; nor does it relieve their feelings of depression over the loss of the marriage. This depression is very common, for although both members of the couple may say openly that they are glad to get rid of the other, there are nevertheless the wasted years of a marriage in which no one was happy; and that loss in itself causes depression. But where there is a child involved, the couple cannot just wash their hands of each other and never have to deal with each other again. Every time the parents look at the child, they will be reminded of their unhappy marriage. Thus, the child's very existence afflicts the divorced couple, who are forced back into hostilities every time something has to be done about child rearing. When there's some kind of decision to be made, it's inconvenient at the least for one divorced parent to have to contact the other—and even more difficult when the divorced couple has to sit down and talk about such problems as orthodontics and who will pay for it. Even if both parents are devoted and well-meaning, with the child's best welfare at heart, they frequently cannot agree because their whole value systems are different—which is why they didn't stay married in the first place.

For an example, take Mr. and Mrs. J. and their 14-year-old son, Ronald.

Before her marriage, Ronald's mother, Lillian, had been a very beautiful woman interested in the fine arts. She had been training as a ballet dancer and hoped for a career until she met her husband Will J. and became pregnant. She wasn't entirely disappointed, however, and looked forward to a happy married life. Though a bright woman, Mrs. J. had little interest in intellectual achievement and had almost failed high school; she cared little about homemaking and, according to her mother, had a long history of being a "sloppy person." She considered (not unreasonably) that the main goal of child rearing was a happy child.

Her husband, on the other hand, was a quite orderly engineer who placed a high value on intellectual achievement. After his marriage, he was shocked to find that his wife did little or no housekeeping. According to his standards, she neglected the child, even though Ronald was always in good health and seemed to thrive. Mr. J. reacted by trying to impose some "discipline" on the boy; his aim was that the child should learn how to perform certain acts as rapidly and efficiently as possible. Mrs. J. complained that her husband was overly demanding and overly strict with the child.

In addition, the couple fought considerably over money: Although Mr. J. made a good salary, the couple made poor investments in their property and in their purchase of stocks, and Mrs. J. was not very good at household management. At the time of the divorce, however, an accounting of their affairs showed that Mr. J. had spent a great deal of income on his cars and his clothes, as compared with the money spent on the household budget itself.

The couple separated when Ronald was four, and were divorced shortly thereafter. Mrs. J. was awarded legal custody of the child, and her husband was obliged to pay several hundred dollars a month child care. Mrs. J. had never worked and had no trade at which to earn any money. She also was awarded the house, but had to make the payments on it. This proved to be a burden, and she used most of the child-care allowance to pay the mortgage. After several years, she fell very far behind on these payments.

Mr. J. used this fact in court as further proof of her wastefulness. Still a beautiful woman, she attracted men but did not remarry. Mr. J. was constantly upset at the thought of other men living in "his" house. Somewhat later, Mr. J. himself remarried, whereupon he sued for a change in custody, claiming that he could offer Ronald a more stable home.

In the meantime, Ronald had become a sickly child for whose many allergies the doctors could find no cause. He was frequently out of school at the slightest excuse, which shocked his father. But since his wife had custody, the school authorities ruled that Mr. J. had no right to the school records. Again he went to his attorney to sue both Mrs. J. and the school, but without success.

At this point he threw up his hands and walked out of the situation, making no child payments for several years. When he returned to the scene, Mrs. J. had convinced Ronald that his father didn't love him and was neglecting him.

Ronald was now at least a year behind in school, a behavior problem both there and at home. But he liked to visit his father, who had moved back into the neighborhood with his new wife. But Ronald utterly refused to come to live with his father. At this point the mother was suing for all the back payments for child care, amounting to far more money than Mr. J. had in his savings; the two parents never spoke. Ronald voluntarily went from one home to another, making demands for money and clothes that were frequently far beyond what either parent could meet. Ronald also brought his problems to both parents, hoping for the most favorable decision.

Whenever Ronald visited his father, he would drop many hints about his mother's behavior that would infuriate the father. Similarly, when Ronald returned home, he would talk about his father's new young wife, which would depress the mother. At Ronald's request his father would buy him sporting equipment and clothes, but would meticulously subtract these expenses from his child-care payments. Often Ronald would disappear for the night with his friends, telling his mother that he was headed to his father's, but would never show up there. If Ronald did visit his father and wanted out for the night, he would merely leave, informing his father that he was returning home.

When Ronald was 14, he finally came to the attention of the Juvenile Court—completely out of parental control, and a heavy user of narcotics. At the child guidance clinic, Ronald admitted having long felt it was his own fault that his parents had divorced in the first place. A failure at school, he felt that neither parent really loved him; he was markedly depressed, almost to the point of suicide.

Unfortunately, such tragedies are prevalent today, beginning immediately at the divorce hearing—or whenever a decision has to be made regarding where the child is to live most of the time.

THE CUSTODY QUESTION

The question of child custody usually creates a considerable amount of conflict. Actually *custody* and *visitation* are terms more legal than meaningful in people's lives. If both parents continue to live in the same community, for example, courts are inclined to grant custody to the mother and allow the father very generous "visitation rights." For most of the week, the child lives with whichever parent is given "custody." At the same time, the parent who doesn't have custody usually has to make some kind of monetary contribution toward the child's care.

In most instances, of course, custody is awarded to the mother, and the father has to make child-care payments. Such payments are customary even if the mother is financially able to support the child entirely on her own. Courts now seem to be giving custody to fathers occasionally, but I have yet to hear of a case in which a mother is making child-care payments to the father.

Thus, the child is likely to continue to live in the same home as before the divorce, and attend the same school. At the same time, his father is likely to see him on the weekends and perhaps spend one evening a week with him.

Since few fathers spend more time with their children anyhow, the chief difference is that the father will be spending it with the child outside of the home. Often the father actually sees his children *more* frequently and is more involved with them than before his divorce—especially if he is the breadwinner. In the majority of instances, on the other hand, divorce means that the mother will have to find work, if she hasn't already done so. Thus, the child may actually see less of the mother, even though she has custody.

Quite often, the parent who is awarded custody is also granted certain legal privileges of decisions about the child's care. Very often, then, the parent granted custody has the right to decide how and where the child will be educated, and to make decisions regarding medical care and residence. Courts are increasingly aware that these decisions cannot always be made unilaterally by one parent, however, particularly if both parents are really concerned with the child's welfare. Thus, where the law allows, courts are increasingly inclined to award "joint" custody, allowing both divorced parents to participate in legal, educational, and medical decisions regarding their children.

In the long run, the main custody conflicts occur over money and child payments. Since money is often the main cause of marital dissension, this issue often remains a bitter dispute after the dissolution of the marriage. Very often a father abandons his children because he feels he no longer has anything to say about their upbringing and is merely handing out money. Only if some equitable resolution of the money issue can be made can other issues be easily resolved.

THE SINGLE PARENT

Although both divorced parents may reside in the same community, it often happens that one parent seldom sees the child, if ever. Quite frequently the father visits the child irregularly, from time to time, and almost unannounced. The mother may feel that he's never really paid much attention to his child's needs and therefore, she has to protect the child herself. In such cases, the father may play little or no significant role in his child's life other than to appear out of nowhere and then disappear again; the child is really reared by a single parent who supplies not only personal care and affection but all the financial support as well. The battering taken by the single parent is in many ways similar to any other parent's, except that the single parent gets a double dose. Thus, the woman who tries to be mother and father finds that her child will be making double demands. The single parent must provide both total affection and total discipline. In this situation, the parent gets little relief and at times, the child makes life quite difficult. For example, if Mother is the sole caretaker and disciplinarian, her child can daydream of an idealized father who would do everything "wonderfully." Some of these daydreams of the perfect parent may be fulfilled when the father comes to take the child off for a pleasant holiday, during which he probably makes few demands on his offspring. Thus, the child perceives the "visiting" parent as permitting all sorts of activities that the "custodial" parent cannot provide or permit on a day-to-day basis.

For example: Jane, age 7, was a petulant, demanding child, and quite a bit overweight. Her mother had a struggle getting Janie to do her homework; the girl also seemed to be helpless in many ways and raised huge fusses over small events. The mother tried to get her to go on a diet, but Janie constantly violated it. Initially, her father made erratic child-care payments and periodic visits, but then disappeared for many months. The mother was forced to take a job she hated, and often she returned home from work with a splitting headache. At this point, Janie's demands and whining seemed impossible.

When the father appeared, he would bring Janie presents and take her off for a long weekend at the beach—during which time Janie didn't have to go to bed on time and could watch TV as long as she wanted. Her father was a charming individual who laughed a great deal and teased and kidded Janie. She adored him. In contrast, her mother was frequently ailing, depressed, and cross.

When the other parent may not be present at all, children frequently imagine an idealized parent, since it is very difficult for them to admit that the vanished parent had actually neglected them. In fact, the fantasized ideal parent is a child's way of denying that he or she has been deserted. When a mother reminds her child that his father has disappeared for good, the child may become angry at her for even suggesting this: "It's *your* fault I don't have a father," Janie would scream.

Children who idealize a visiting parent often look forward to the weekend. When mother and child are at odds during the week, quite often the child will shout, "Just wait till the weekend!" meaning that the father will then be more permissive. The mother fears this because she knows the child does need *some* discipline. Feeling burdened by her day-to-day responsibilities, she may actually look forward to a day or two off when her ex-husband takes over. In turn, the father does want to be liked by a child he hasn't seen for a week—and whom he really may not know too well, particularly if one reason for his divorce was that he was too busy to play an active role in his child's life. Thus, the visiting parent may find himself with only a weekend to entertain an unhappy child with whom he's only slightly acquainted.

The battering taken by the visiting parent (usually the father) is not always quite as open and direct as the conflicts between child and custodial parent—but often equally devastating, nevertheless. He now has the child for the weekend, perhaps one other day a week, and has to think up something to do with this kid. He doesn't realize that the child thinks he is going to be Santa Claus. Moreover, he may have other commitments besides the child. If he thinks that he's going to share the child with his girl friend, his golf game, or his business, he may be sadly mistaken. Likely his child will be bored at best—but more often will be petulant, demanding, and impatient, if not outright angry.

Other fathers may feel that they have to make up for not being present in the child's daily life—and thus become weekend disciplinarians. They want to investigate the child's school achievement, religious training, and progress in music or sports, just when the child looks forward to a free weekend of relaxation and pleasure. Far too often, the desperate father looks to his girl friend as an assistant baby-sitter or farms the child out to his parents so that *he* can have a weekend free. Girl friends are likely to become obstinate about such an arrangement and refuse to care for another woman's child. Grandparents may be a bit more tolerant, but find the child whiny and disappointed that the father isn't around.

And so the visits gradually diminish. The father "cannot make it," and on the weekend, when he might be visiting, the children find other things to do. Thus, it becomes mutually inconvenient to carry out the visitation program. The visiting parent may blame the custodial parent for influencing the child—who, of course, comes home and complains about the visit. The custodial parent, fearing the worst, blames the ex-spouse. A vicious circle is set up with ensuing lawsuits, each parent blaming the other, with the child in the middle.

"YOU'RE JUST LIKE YOUR FATHER [OR MOTHER]"

Although a couple's separation may be decreed by law, unfortunately, their feelings are not shut off. And child-parent conflicts in the divorced family can become even more bitter and hostile if the child comes to represent to either parent the unwanted and unhappy marriage. There is the living reminder and image of the divorced spouse, the person the single parent has come to hate. The child often has the same speech, gestures, and personality characteristics. Every time the parent is angry at the child, it's very tempting to double the anger by recalling the old wounds of the divorce.

Of course the child cannot quite understand why the parent should get so extremely angry over what might otherwise have been a relatively innocuous misdemeanor. Particularly right after a divorce, a parent is likely to be depressed and thus be unduly harsh in discipline (especially if discipline has been neglected during the marital breakup). If the mother inadvertently remarks, "You're just like your father," the boy or girl is likely to feel even more rejected, knowing how much the mother hates the father. In a very likely reaction-formation to this situation, the child becomes doubly angry back at the parent. Thus, after a divorce, a previously well-behaved child may become exceedingly impudent, disobedient, even delinquent. The sweet child will become more passive, the playful child more mischievous, the frail child more sickly.

Quite often one parent still retains a great deal of fondness for the other, mixed with a great deal of anger. Thus, a divorced father may still be quite in love with his ex-wife and be angry chiefly because—for reasons he cannot understand—he is rejected and his love is not returned. This may complicate relationships between the child and the parent who is still carrying the torch. If a woman's husband has taken off with some other woman and she can't understand at all why she has been rejected *and* continues to be in love with her husband despite their divorce, she may have a far different relationship with his child. Every time she looks up at her son, she may see in him her lost lover. At times she may react in a very seductive fashion; at others she may take out her anger at being rejected by her husband on his son.

Similar reactions are common between a father and his daughter in whom he sees the girl he was in love with, the girl he married, the girl who walked off with some other man. His daughter may not understand why he sometimes acts in an erotic manner toward her but at other moments is unduly and constantly angry at her. Usually quite confused by this reaction, a child may try to separate from the parent who's acting in this crazy fashion. Or if the child does feel overwhelmed by the parent's attempts to reconstitute a love affair using the child as the love object, he or she is likely to try to move away from such a seductive, erotic situation. When the parent is angry over something that may seem like nothing and feels hurt at every little rejection, the puzzled child may also try to withdraw. Then, of course, the parent reacting in this way is likely to be doubly hurt, and relive the rejection felt in the first place from the divorced and deserting spouse.

On the other hand, if the child *doesn't* make efforts to separate from the heartbroken and deserted parent, then a very difficult and neurotic relationship becomes established. The child becomes increasingly entangled in an unnatural relationship with the parent, and often will later develop no outside love life of his or her own. For example: Vivian, almost 12, was quite astounded when her parents separated, because she had never heard them quarrel. When her father moved out, she continued to live with her mother. She then became aware that her mother had a lover, who often visited the home. Her mother went away on dates or even for whole weekends with him.

Vivian saw her father every weekend and often during the week, too: When her mother was away, her father often came back and stayed, taking care of Vivian. He continued to refer to the house as *his* home and kept on doing a great deal of the gardening and upkeep. He adored Vivian and often remarked how much she looked like her mother. He let his daughter know that he was exceedingly unhappy and still was very fond of her mother—in fact, he openly wept in front of Vivian over the fact that her mother had deserted him for another man.

The girl felt very sorry for her father and, after the weekend, would berate her mother for not having any more affection for him. Vivian's mother found it exceedingly difficult to explain her side of the story. Vivian became more and more defiant of her mother and often refused to obey her. She started failing at school, quarreling with many of her former friends, and seemed to have little or no social life. Rather, she would frequently telephone her father and spend extra afternoons or evenings with him.

Vivian's mother was upset but made no strong objections; she thought it best to just let the girl have her way and hoped the situation would eventually remedy itself. After the divorce was final and the mother proposed to marry her boyfriend, Vivian became exceedingly upset. The girl then decided to go live with her father, although her mother tried to countermand this entirely. Then Vivian's father sued for review of the custody situation: Now that Vivian was of an age where the court respected her viewpoint, she was allowed to go live with the father.

For a while she seemed very happy in this setting, doing all the housework, cooking for her father, and in fact playing housewife to him. Her mother worried because Vivian seemed to have little social life of her own. Rather, throughout her teenage years she was busy housekeeping and going places and doing things with her father. She became extremely religious and decided at one point to become a nun. After a brief time as a novitiate, however, she returned from the convent because her father was ill.

After completing high school, under her mother's

pressure—and in agreement with the father—she did go away to college. At this time, her father remarried. However, Vivian seemed discontented at college and came back to live with her father and new stepmother. Initially she got along well with her stepmother, although the stepmother felt that Vivian was frequently under foot and took over many of the duties, such as the cooking and house care, that the stepmother had assumed would be hers. Moreover, Vivian's room was filled with pictures of her mother; several times the stepmother saw her husband in Vivian's room staring at the pictures of his ex-wife.

Gradually there ensued more and more quarrels between the father and the stepmother over many little things—but often involving Vivian. Vivian felt very innocent of this and often returned to her room to cry because she felt she had caused the father and stepmother's quarrels in some way. Finally the father and stepmother separated, and Vivian again was left to be housekeeper to her father. He developed a bizarre illness that could not be diagnosed but required him to be sedentary, and was finally unable to work at all. Luckily there was still enough income for the two of them. Vivian devoted the next 15 years to her father's care, until his death. At age 45 she was unmarried and quite neurotic.

Since a child cannot be a satisfactory adult lover in any sense, the parent will continue to be depressed and disappointed. Usually, as in Vivian's case, a very unnatural, possessive relationship develops: The child feels bound to answer every parental whim, and the parent is never satisfied. Quite often, both parent and child end up as a severely emotionally disturbed pair living exceedingly unhappy lives.

DIVORCES WITHOUT VICTIMS

Although it is doubtful that a divorce can occur without some feelings of hurt, disappointment, and anger, such feeling need not become aggrandized into a tragedy. It *is* quite possible to get a divorce without extreme rancor, and for a divorced couple to carry on the job of being parents despite their marriage's dissolution.

Such a happy turn of events requires considerable efforts and good intentions by both parties. First, it's essential that when it comes to the care of the children, neither divorced party starts blaming the other. It cannot be overemphasized that *blame does not help anyone.* The parents who pay little attention to the child's needs and only to their own hurt feelings are most likely to be battered. Each parent must be dedicated to the child's welfare. Even more, he or she must grant that the divorced spouse has the same interests in mind. When divorced parents are to deal with the problems the child presents, angers and rancor must be set aside.

This is very difficult to do at times and often requires the intervention of a third party. In most instances, unfortunately, the courts do not provide any kind of counseling for divorced parents; and the idea of post-divorce counseling for children and parents is relatively new. However, there need not be a continuance of marital hostilities; in fact the divorce was intended to *end* such hostilities. Particularly in the case of divorce, parents must learn to handle hurt feelings, as discussed in Chapter 5.

14. THE STEPPARENT TRAP

In literature and in legends around the world, stepparents have traditionally been portrayed as unfeeling and rejecting, if not actively cruel and vicious. Since legends are usually perpetuated as an illustration of the mores of any particular society, there must have been some purpose to these myths at one time.

The legend of the evil stepparent originated in centuries when parents were lost chiefly through death; the death rate of women during childbirth was particularly high and men often remarried—especially to widows—in order to have the children taken care of. Exactly why stepparents were depicted in this manner is long lost in antiquity, but two main purposes seem probable. First, children were ever being warned that they might lose their parents if they didn't behave themselves, and thus stepparents were portrayed as the evil substitutions. This legend may have also been aimed as a warning to the stepparents themselves, to assume a kindly role and not neglect or be cruel to the child.

Actually, such tales serve yet a third purpose in a culture: the depiction of prevalent underlying feelings that must be taken into account. *Cinderella* does not at all represent what stepparents are really like, but rather how children may *regard* stepparents. In the days of predominantly autocratic parents, discipline and punishment often could be quite cruel. Children often were given heavy workloads, and one child might easily be favored over another. However, these situations were often highly exaggerated in the stepchild's mind.

There may have at one time been some fact as well as fiction in *Cinderella,* but of course the evil witch is entirely Snow White's delusion. Stories such as *Cinderella* or *Snow White* are such exaggerations that they place even the good-intentioned stepparent in serious jeopardy. On the basis of these legends children learn to *expect* cruelty from their stepparents.

The point is that children create a stepparent image in reaction to the loss of a biological parent. The Cinderella legend thus illustrates some of the main feelings that children have about stepparents. In the first place, Cinderella feels rejected and jealous because her stepmother has intervened between herself and her beloved father and stolen away the father's love. Next, the stepmother is shown as favoring her own daughters over poor Cinderella. The stepmother and stepsisters are depicted as jealous. However, Cinderella is depicted as not at all resentful or jealous—merely hurt. Here the child avoids the "sin" of jealousy by projecting this naughty feeling into the stepparent and stepsiblings. Most of all, the stepmother is depicted as being unfair in her allotment of household chores.

Far deeper and more murderous feelings are depicted

in *Snow White*, where the evil witch stepmother seeks the very life of the innocent child by hiring a hunter to cut out her heart. In both legends, the stepchild is to be pitied and no mention is made of the possibility of the stepchild having angry, resentful, or jealous feelings. Obviously, these legends portray how children feel about stepparents so that both stepparents and biological parents can take such feelings into account.

Actually, children's feelings about stepparents are even more extensive and conflictual than suggested by either of these famous stories. Indeed, the stepparent legend is an integral part of children's imaginations regarding their *own* parents. It is an almost universal fantasy among children at times that their alleged mother and father are, in reality, not their parents at all. Particularly when the child feels abused by disciplining parents, the child fantasies that the "real" parents have been abducted and foster parents have been substituted. This fantasy is also depicted in literature and is a common theme in both Greek and Shakespearian plays. Even where the real parents are still alive and there is no divorce, the child may well create a fantasy about being reared by stepparents.

When marital tensions boil over to threaten the marriage, the possibility of the stepparent fantasy becoming reality rises strongly in the child's mind. If the child is aware of either parent being involved in an extra-marital affair then his fear of the stepparent fantasy may be strongly aroused. But even when there is no third party before the divorce, children often begin (almost at the time of the separation) to imagine what it will be like when a parent remarries. After a while many children actually voice the hope that the parent *will* remarry, particularly if the parent is using the child as a substitute spouse. But feelings about a mother remarrying are often ambivalent.

The boy who finds himself without a male role model but who has a close and intimate relationship with his mother may actually seek a man who would marry her. At other moments, the same boy may just as likely decide to possess his mother for himself and drive away any prospective husbands.

A boy doesn't seem to be as bothered by his father's girl friends unless he is living with his father and sees his female friends as potential stepmothers who will discipline and intervene in their father-son relationship. If a girl is living with her mother, she may actually encourage her to remarry, hoping to share the affections of the new husband/father. Such a hope will be even stronger if the biological father is no longer in the picture. But whether or not they are living with their fathers, daughters are even more jealous of potential stepmothers.

For example: When Amy was 3 and her sister, Alma, was 5, their mother suffered a severe depression. The children did not see her during the almost two years she spent in a mental hospital. She returned briefly, but then left the family without notice and again disappeared. During the next two years of her absence the father and the two girls became very close. The father, too, was at least mildly depressed and did not seek the companionship of any other woman, always hoping that his wife would recover. Most of his life was bound up in the care of these two girls, who dominated his life. He made few demands on them and jokingly agreed that they were both spoiled. At the same time, he was quite overprotective and anxious lest he make some error in raising them. There he was, Johnny-on-the-spot for every one of their needs, at the cost of any of his own pleasures or activities.

He was so fussy about the girls' care that his live-in housekeepers frequently quit. The girls became very demanding and obstreperous, in trouble at school because they didn't obey the teacher or do their work. Fortunately, they were very bright and grasped their lessons almost immediately, but this only gave them a further impression that there was no need to struggle or wait for anything. They were also very attractive girls who could be quite charming, which also aided them in getting by.

The father had been excessively bitter when his wife

deserted them, and two years later his anger increased when he discovered she was filing for divorce so she could marry another man. The girls also were openly angry at their mother, telling everyone in earshot what a "bitch" she was. A year later, when their father met Audrey, the girls seemed to like her and enjoyed being with her. Audrey, who was 25 (ten years younger than their father) was really like a big sister to these nearly pubescent girls, and they had lots of fun together at the beach, riding horses, and shopping.

The girls were quite cool, however, to the idea that Audrey might marry their father and come to live with them as a stepmother. Initially charmed by these physically active and beautiful girls, Audrey had no children from her previous, unhappy teenage marriage. She saw these two little girls as needing a mother and was determined to become mother and psychotherapist to them.

But, as might be expected, Audrey's hopes of reforming these two headstrong youngsters were quickly dashed. At her wedding, these two girls actually told her that they hated her and would never accept her. Audrey did not give up easily and kept attempting to win their favor, but without success. When she attempted to discipline them, they openly defied her. They began to play little tricks on her, clung more closely to their father, and used all of their best wiles to set him against Audrey, who was soon quarreling with her husband. After less than a year, Audrey moved out of the house, challenging the husband to leave the children—which, of course, he did not do.

Rightly or wrongly, the child is likely to view the *potential* stepparent as the cause of the marital disruption and as an enemy. The blame for any ensuing breakup and unhappiness will fall on the interloper. This is often reinforced by the offended parent who, when left for someone else, lets the child know how unhappy he or she is. All this places the potential stepparent in a very difficult position.

Stepparents suffer another bad mark in that they

become "proof positive" of the divorce. Children cling to the hope that no matter what the judge has said, some day the parents will reunite. If one of the parents remarries, this shatters the child's hope. This makes the stepparent a double interloper; he or she has not only taken away the parent's love, but has destroyed all hopes of a parental reunion. Thus, whatever the stepparent's intention or hope, he or she may be battered merely because of the child's expectations and attitudes. The child says, in effect, "You are not my parent" and stoutly maintains that he or she already has parents and does not need any more. The child may thus be prepared to engage in battle against the stepparent no matter what.

"YOU CAN'T TELL ME WHAT TO DO"

Well-behaved children are likely to reveal their negative feelings about a stepparent by foot-dragging. They will engage in activity with the stepparent only with obvious reluctance, or not allow the new parent to assume any parental obligations. Not only will the children resist discipline, but may also evade any efforts to be taken care of by giving the stepparent the cold shoulder. It's surprising how often such relationships—which may have been smooth or even pleasant before the actual marriage—change character once the new relationship becomes formalized and permanent. Rarely do children accept the stepparent in any way other than begrudgingly. The most usual statement is "He [or she] is all right, I *guess*."

If the stepparent also tries to stay in the background and avoid a relationship, a cold war with the child may ensue and become increasingly intense. But when the stepparent makes any attempt to assume a parental role, particularly to share in the discipline of the child, open warfare is likely to break out. "You can't tell me what to do" becomes the child's watchword. Often, parents remarry to get some help in raising the children. A mother may remarry in order to provide her son with a role model and for additional help in the discipline. Similarly, a father may feel the need of a woman to raise his daughters. Since children usually resent discipline (especially punishment) this adds to the string of resentment against the stepparent. The stepparent who tries to lay down the law may meet with a more widespread, and heated, rebellion than might be shown toward a natural parent.

Quite often the stepparent's position becomes even more precarious because of actions by the natural parents. Even if the "custodial" parent has sought a spouse to help control, it's frequently difficult for the natural parent to hand over discipline to the stepparent. The natural parent may want the new mate's assistance and support, but may not give the new spouse the prerogative to initiate any discipline. Thus, the stepparent is in a difficult role: being expected to act like a parent, but not granted the authority. This is especially true when the stepparent comes along late in the picture, after the natural parent has been single for some time. This situation can be quite difficult, since neither child nor parent is willing to relinquish his or her role totally.

"YOU LOVE YOUR CHILDREN BETTER"

Whenever the stepparent has biological children, the steprelationship becomes even more complicated. In the single-child nuclear family, the relationship is three-sided: between each parent and between each parent and the child. This relationship becomes six-sided when there are two children, and progresses geometrically with each additional child. In the stepparent family, when there is one child involved, it becomes six- or seven-sided: The child relates to each of the biological parents and to the stepparent. The biological parent and the new mate also have a relationship, and there is usually a remnant of relationship between the divorced parents over the child. Moreover, it is not uncommon for stepparents to have some kind of relationship with the ex-spouse—often a negative relationship, which is another reason the child may hold a grudge against the stepparent.

One often sees a stepparent blaming the natural spouse for all the child's misbehaviors. Yet the self-righteous stepparent who attempts to reform the child from the influence of the neurotic predecessor is likely to run into trouble from the start.

When stepsisters and stepbrothers are involved, the number of potential relationships becomes almost out of reach. Not that stepbrothers and stepsisters may not form close and intimate friendships, sometimes more friendly than between biological siblings. However, the "Cinderella syndrome" is quite common. The child feels that the stepparent favors his or her own children, even when the stepparent may be doing the utmost to be fair. Just as sibling rivalry often sharpens in a hostile marriage, it becomes overwhelming in a hostile divorce. Warfare among stepsisters and stepbrothers can often be very intense and disruptive; again the poor stepparent gets blamed.

This rivalry is more intense when the child has expected the new stepparent to be some kind of idealized parent who will take the place of the lost biological parent. Of course, no stepmother can ever replace the idealized "angel" mother who died and thus deserted the child. More likely, the child will project onto the stepmother the anger he felt at being deserted. Similarly, the stepfather will have great difficulty in replacing the "ideal" who may have indeed deserted the child long ago. The child who says, "You love yours better than me" may really mean "I expected to get all of your love," and working these problems out may be very difficult.

In addition, stepsiblings are likely to look to the child's biological parent for very similar affection—and with very similar conflictual and negative feelings. It's thus natural for newly remarried partners to retreat a bit from the attacks of each other's respective stepchildren and to turn a bit more to their own biological offspring. If a parent is loved by one child and hated by another, it's only natural to turn to the child who shows the most affection. Trying to develop an equally affectionate relationship with a stepchild does require considerably high motivation.

REVERSING THE LEGEND

Perhaps stepparents are always going to be at some disadvantage. The conflicts inherent in this situation are seldom completely resolved, and may in fact not be fully resolvable. Yet people commonly remarry in order to get help in rearing children and, conversely, other people marry people with children because they want to be parents. The stepparent role can be most positive if *both* stepparent and stepchild recognize this relationship as unique and different from other kinds of parent-child relationships. A stepparent does not need to be forced into the evil role of legend, but may create a new and special and enjoyable relationship. The creation of this relationship requires the biological parent's continued support.

For example: Shortly before Christmas, Ronnie, age 12, and his sister, Valerie, 10, were standing at the window as their mother backed the car down the snowy driveway to the street. She had the windows rolled up, the heater and radio on, and didn't hear the firetruck that crashed into her car, killing her in front of the children.

For the following year, their father and these two children gathered themselves together in an increasing closeness and intimacy. Their grief was so strong that a year later, all the mother's possessions, even her toothbrush, lay exactly where she had left them. Every night the father and the children would stand on the porch and look at the stars in a grief-stricken ceremony, remembering their lost mother.

Ronnie papered over the window where he was standing when the mother's car was hit so that he could no longer see out. Both children ate constantly, and Valerie became quite obese. Yet she would not allow anyone to buy her new clothes and if permitted, would have continued to wear day and night the dress she was wearing when her mother was killed.

Mr. R's sister and his mother both advised him that his children's grief was excessive. He began to see for himself that some alterations were necessary. He sought my advice, and we held a series of family meetings in which more grief was spoken out, and they even voiced some of their anger over being deserted. A summer away at the grandmother's home also helped, and the following September, the children seemed to be making better progress at school again. I also counseled the father to find activities for himself outside the home. He began attending a single parent's group where he met Veta, who was approximately his age and had two daughters in their early teens. The two families began spending their weekends together alternating between the two homes. Veta was divorced and her children visited their father frequently, so that Mr. R., Ronnie, Valerie, and Veta would be together on alternate weekends. In dealing with Ronnie and Valerie, Veta was extremely cautious and gentle. She seemed to understand and accept their prolonged grief and made no demands on them.

When Mr. R. asked her to help him select some new clothes for Valerie, she suggested that maybe Valerie wasn't ready for her to take on such a task, and that it would be more proper for the aunt or grandmother to do this at that time. These words were spoken in front of Valerie, who responded shyly that she would like Veta to help her choose some new clothes. Veta and her two daughters were on a diet, and Valerie was able to join them and lose some weight.

Veta also requested to be included in the family counseling sessions, saying that if she were to play the role of stepmother, she wanted to be able to understand the children's feelings. Here again, however, she was very careful not to intrude into their feelings but sat back, silently listening rather than being at all invasive. In these counseling sessions, the role she might play as a stepmother was gradually defined by the children, by the father, and by Veta herself.

In the last several sessions before Mr. R. married Veta, her children also were included in these counseling sessions, and we also explored what kind of relationships could be expected between the stepsiblings.

At this time, the new couple were planning their new home—which had to be much larger than either home to accommodate a family of six. The planning of the new home became a communal project, involving both members of the couple and their four children. Thus, the new family started off on a fresh foot, with openness and tenderness among them.

The remaining problem was Ronnie, who did feel left out of the trinity of girls. He withdrew more and more into his own room, which was dominated by a large picture of his mother. But he devoted himself to his studies and became an outstanding scholar. He was a slightly built boy who had little or no interest in athletics and thus had few peer acquaintances. The new home had a swimming pool, and the father encouraged him to become a good competitive swimmer.

However, it was only several years later that Ronnie began to come out of what had been a prolonged adolescent depression. Once he entered college he seemed to find himself, gathering extra rewards from his peers in his scholastic achievements and challenge in his schoolwork. On his first vacation home from college, he approached Veta and told her how much he loved her and thanked her for being so patient with him.

Suffice it to say that it can seldom be taken for granted that a child will be completely happy with the new stepparent. If someone who doesn't want or like children is foolish enough to marry another person who already has children, their marriage is likely to be short-lived. While there are definite negative components in the step-relationship, there are also very positive factors that can be played upon and emphasized to create a positive, supportive relationship. For example, the boy who has no father and badly wants one and the man who doesn't have a son and desires one may form a close and warm relationship—despite the factors mentioned above. If the positive motivations and feelings are to be realized, however, it's usually necessary to resolve some of these negative factors.

Disabusing the child of these feelings and creating a positive relationship often requires considerable time and patience. It involves the understanding of the child's feelings in considerable detail. Most of all, such resolutions of these step-conflicts require the cooperation and full efforts of the biological parents as well.

The first step is to recognize that negative factors *are* present. The wise stepparent—and biological parent—has to realize that the child may not accept the new marriage initially. Both must allow these negative feelings and, to a certain extent, let them run their course. A stepparent cannot expect to have a buddy-buddy step-relationship right away. The biological parent in particular must realize that the child may blame the stepparent for the divorce, and it's the biological parent's duty to let the child know that there may have been many other reasons. The biological parent must take the responsibility for the separation; he or she must tell the child, "Look, your stepparent did not force me to divorce your mother (or father); it was *my* decision. I fell in love with your stepparent and was no longer in love with your mother (or father)."

This message may need to be repeated several times, in different forms, at different times. The biological parent must also grant that the child *need not* necessarily love the stepparent, saying in effect, "Yes, I love my new husband (or wife). However, you need not love the same person I love. Just as I no longer love your mother (or father), you have my full permission to continue to love that other person." Such statements in various forms help to reassure the child that there will be no loss of love, nor any demand for love.

A third and most important message from the biological parent is that new love for the stepparent does not mean that there is any less love for the child. The biological parent must say and demonstrate repeatedly, "I can and do love both of you." Finally the biological parent must say to the child, over and over again, "When you are living with me, your stepparent is an equal parent with me, and must be regarded with the same respect if not the same affection."

The biological parent must constantly support the stepparent in all attempts at playing the parental role. The biological parent must encourage and share with the stepparent the enjoyable parental roles of playing with and caring for the child, and similarly, support the stepparent in the role of disciplinarian. Only through such support has the stepparent any chance of being a successful parent. Where there are children from both previous marriages, then this agreement to share parenting for both sets of children must be a mutual one. It follows that the new couple should come to some general agreement on what behavior is desired. Any divorced person seeking a spouse must make sure that the new partner has similar sets of values regarding child raising, or the second marriage may be doomed. It would also help if new parents could agree to disagree—if they may not totally agree, they should at least get together and support each other. Each should say to the other (out of the child's hearing): "You may insist on certain behavior from the child, even though I wouldn't." Of course, if the two parents expect diverse or opposite kinds of behavior, they must resolve these differences.

Again, the stepparent has a much better chance of a positive and meaningful step-relationship if he or she adopts a democratic approach to childrearing. The stepparent who disciplines through praise and reward rather than exclusively through punishment is going to find a child much more receptive. It must be emphasized that discipline does not necessarily involve punishment; a great deal of parental guidance is carried out by encouragement, rewards, and praise. Thus a stepparent can best get a child's cooperation by these same positive methods. The stepparent who enjoys the task of caring for and guiding the child also will be much less battered.

Most difficult for the stepparent, of course, is to accept that he or she is not the "real parent" but rather fulfills a very special role, distinct from that of a biological parent. The person who can feel comfortable in this special role is much more likely to succeed. Not pretending to take the lost parent's place, the stepparent will rather say in effect to the child, "Look, I am a stepparent. I'm a different person than the parent you lost, probably a different parent than you expected. You and I have a special relationship." You may note that this message is very similar to that suggested in books directed to adoptive and foster parents. In effect, the stepparent *is* an adoptive parent—if not necessarily legally. Openly acknowledging this special parenthood clears the way for a new and different, yet meaningful, step-relationship.

15. EPILOGUE: THE JOY OF PARENTING

Alex Comfort writes of the "Joy of Sex," but the physical creation of a child is but a fleeting moment—far too often a feckless moment, and the fact of pregnancy is usually more sobering news. Yet the prospect of having a child is often joyous for those who have been hoping for one. Even those who have *not* planned on being parents often greet the fact of pregnancy with some mixed feelings of pleasure. In working with unmarried girls, who are ill-prepared to become mothers and who agree to give up their children for adoption, counselors often run into difficulty because the girl alternates between being "reasonable" and giving up the child, and being "emotional" by expressing a desire to keep her baby. Thus most

184

children who are kept by their mothers are wanted; and any rejecting feelings are secondary and usually repressed.

Pregnancy, for all the physical distress that it entails, is a time of happy expectancy for many women. In fact it is usually the overly anxious and doubtful woman who suffers physically. For many, pregnancy is a few months of peaceful contentment, even though their bodies give them moments of extreme discomfort. Although the joy of pregnancy comes largely from the expectation, women have told me that they like being pregnant, that they experience a physical and psychological sensation of fulfillment and repose that no man can understand. The mixture of pleasure and pain heightens the overall emotional experience of bearing a child. This feminine emotional experience is conveyed to the husband in laughter and tears, often without an immediate reason, so that he, too, enjoys the wife's pregnancy. He experiences, perhaps vicariously, a joy in her vivaciousness, her alternate moments of tranquillity, and the happiness her eyes, her voice, her gestures convey. She is often most beautiful during pregnancy, her skin most clear, her laughter heightened, her attention most rapturous. During the final months of pregnancy their sexual contacts are limited, but there's no question that a woman's physical and psychological affection for her husband is usually stronger during pregnancy than at any other time. Only the most "macho" or childish man resents or rejects a pregnant wife.

The birth of a child is usually a time for celebration. In a few hours the physical pain comes to a grand climax. Surprisingly (to a man), women usually do not complain of childbirth, and if they do remember the labor pains they smile as they speak of it. The easy, anesthetized births seem the least memorable.

The months of pregnancy, however, are a tiny fraction of the time and energy devoted to being a parent. The *real* labor of parenting begins when the child and mother come home from the hospital. As described in Chapter 2, caring for the newborn is a 24-hour job, but, for most parents, this constant attention is equaled by a constant pleasure. Feeding, bathing, rocking, cuddling baby may occupy most of mother's time, with little or no time for the father when he is home, but who would give up these tasks, even the 2:00 A.M. feeding? Holding baby to the breast—and to the father's chest—is a supreme joy. Perhaps soiled diapers are abhorrent to squeamish young parents, but even they laugh about it. Sometimes the mother leaves the task of changing baby to father. "The top half is mine and the bottom half his" joked one young mother; her husband winked and smiled as if he were glad to be involved in some manner with the care of the newborn.

The *work* of parenting has been described in detail throughout this book; I hope that I have also mentioned the rewards. Parenting grows more complex with each step of the child's development, but the pleasure also develops and increases. Watching a child grow, watching the child crawl or take his or her first step and first pratfall, make the first meaningful sound, respond to the parent's voice, and even repel parent's attention—all fill the parent's heart with great joy.

Some books describe the "terrible two's": the toddler says "no!" before yes; the toddler is into everything. A 3- or 4-year-old needs watching, running after, and restricting. But now the baby responds—even to discipline—with hugs and kisses. The child's achievements in speech, in motor skills, in observing and relating, all provide proud moments for both parents.

The preschooler's endless repetitive "Why?" drives parents crazy, but their egos are inflated as they become the authorities for their child's perception of the world. Teaching, guiding, disciplining a child may seem an endless task for which the reward is not immediate. But every parent's heart leaps when a neighbor reports, "You have a well-behaved child," especially when a parent fears that none of the discipline seems to have taken hold.

This book has outlined some of the major "battles"

between parent and child, especially ones that leave parents psychologically "battered." Yet parents who endure these battles, who take the time and trouble to discipline and train a child, win in the long run. Again, Democratic Parenting requires more work and more energy, but it is ever a creative job. Being a parent is a bit like being a sculptor. There is a constant chipping away, a shaping, a polishing, then more refining. But the result is a live and responding human being. Statues give no affection; they do not grow or achieve. No Mona Lisa equals the charm, vivaciousness, or the exuberance of a sixteen-year-old girl; or the energy, thoughtlessness, and thoughtfulness of an adolescent boy. Teenagers are always a moving picture, that stir parental emotions, positively and negatively, almost at the same moment. "That child!" the parent exclaims in exasperation, but with a smile.

It is this mixture of emotions, this intertwining of fear and hope, of joy and anger, of pain and pleasure that makes parenthood so excruciatingly joyful. In the midst of some momentary battle, when the results are almost too distant to imagine, the child is sent off to her or his room screaming and in tears, but when the silence falls, the parents know that they have done "the right thing," and will, if necessary, go through it again the next day and the next, as long as the child's behavior requires it.

The greatest pain and pleasure occur at the conclusion of child rearing, when the young adult leaves the nest. The job is over; the parents have done their best, and are not needed as parents any longer.

Not that there is no affection between the parent and the adult son or daughter, but the affection is different. It is an affectionate "Thank you"—along with the "No, thank you" of being separate and not needing parental guidance. The adult makes no demand on the parent, but cannot in good conscience yield to parental demands.

Yet even this resulting "separation anxiety" is not only endurable, but a final fulfillment of the parental role—if the parents have been preparing for it, have encouraged their child to take independent steps, to accept increasing responsibility, to venture further from parental control and advice. Parents can and should take increasing pride in that. The young adult finally does everything without parental attention. Although parents experience the greatest pleasure when their offspring become famous, achieve high professional status, or become financially well-off, pleasure also comes when sons or daughters achieve even modest success, create happy marriages, and have children of their own in their quest to be successful parents themselves.

Index

Index